Roman Catholic/Lutheran Joint Commission

FACING UNITY

Models, Forms and Phases
of Catholic-Lutheran Church Fellowship

Published by
The Lutheran World Federation
1985

Parallel issue in German

Einheit vor uns
(Verlag Bonifatius-Druckerei Paderborn/Verlag Otto Lembeck,
Frankfurt am Main, 1980)

ISBN 2 88190 000 3
(ISBN 3 87088 438 X Verlag Bonifatius - German Edition)
(ISBN 3 87476 231 9 Verlag Lembeck - German Edition)

Contents

A. FACING UNITY

B. EXCURSUS

C. MARTIN LUTHER –
WITNESS TO JESUS CHRIST

*Statement by the Roman Catholic-Lutheran Joint Commission
on the occasion of Martin Luther's 500th birthday*

A.

FACING UNITY

Preface

Unity in the truth, the elimination of divisive differences, and thus the achievement of church fellowship — these have been and are the main concerns in the dialogue initiated in 1967 between the Lutheran World Federation and the Roman Catholic Church.

With the publication of the Malta Report "The Gospel and the Church" in 1972, a first round of discussions was completed. This established an extensive consensus in the interpretation of justification and also a convergence of views in the controversial question of the relationship between Scripture and Tradition.

With a view to settling problems which it had been impossible to deal with adequately in the Malta Report, a new stage of the dialogue was launched. In 1978, the Roman Catholic/Lutheran Joint Commission was able to adopt the statement on *The Eucharist* in which serious differences were eliminated and a common witness formulated in fundamental questions. In 1981, the document *The Ministry in the Church* was published which shows convergences and agreements in the understanding of the common priesthood, the ordained ministry, ordination, and the apostolic succession.

A year earlier, in 1980, there had been the common statement on the *Confessio Augustana* — the basic confession of all Lutheran churches. On the basis of an evaluation of careful studies, the Commission was able to affirm that we are "all under one Christ". For it was not only the declared intention of the Augsburg Confession of 1530 to remain in accord with the faith of the Early Church and the Roman Church: its statements in great measure realize this intention. The "newly discovered agreement in central Christian truths" gave "good ground for the hope that in the light of this basic consensus answers will also be forthcoming to the still unsettled questions and problems, answers which will achieve the degree of unanimity required if our churches are to make a decisive advance from their present state of division to that of sister churches" (*All Under One Christ,* 25).

In 1983, the 500th anniversary of the birth of Martin Luther provided the opportunity for a joint statement "Martin Luther — Witness to Jesus Christ".

The documents and statements just mentioned served indirectly the goal of church fellowship. The latter was dealt with directly and explicitly in a document, *Ways to Community,* published in 1980. "Christian Unity is a blessing of the Triune God, a work which he accomplishes, by means he chooses, in ways he determines" (*Ways to Community,* 8). These considerations proceed from the unity already given in Christ, focus attention on the barriers which still remain and point out what is already now possible and necessary; they encourage us to take those steps together which can bring us nearer to the goal.

Finally, in 1984 the Commission completed its work on a document on which it had worked for many years: *Facing Unity — Models, Forms and Phases of Catholic-Lutheran Church Fellowship.* This document strives for clarity regarding the nature of church unity and a concept of that goal which implies neither absorption nor return, but rather a structured fellowship of churches. The prerequisite is community in confessing the one faith and in sacramental life. A solution must be found for still existing divisive differences. The dialogue documents require to be examined, perhaps corrected and supplemented, and finally given authority in the churches. This is a condition for complete church fellowship in word, sacrament and ministry. The document presented here seeks to outline step by step how such church fellowship could become a reality. The Commission is conscious that the latter part of its considerations, in particular, is venturesome and provisional in character. We have always to remain open for God's ways and dispensations. All our reflections are, in the end, "a prayer to the Lord who knows ways which surpass our vision and are beyond our power", as the document says in conclusion.

Rome, 3rd March 1984

Hans L. Martensen	George A. Lindbeck
Bishop of Copenhagen	Professor, Yale University
Denmark	USA

co-chairmen

Introduction

1. The full realization of unity given in Christ and promised by him calls for concrete forms of ecclesial life in common. Of what sort could and should these be? What is their relationship to our present ecclesial realities? What challenges are connected with this? What concrete steps have to be taken? We pose these questions by considering in Part I the key term "models of unity", and in the light of our substantially common understanding of the nature of unity we examine the forms or models of church unity found in the history of the church, particularly the recent ecumenical discussions. In Part II we deal specifically with the relationship between the Roman Catholic Church and the Lutheran churches and with the question of forms and phases of Catholic-Lutheran church fellowship.

Part I

Concept of Unity and Models of Union

2. For us "models of union" are not arbitrary constructions. We see in them realizable forms of the fundamental understanding of unity described in our document *Ways to Community* (Roman Catholic/Lutheran Joint Commission, Geneva 1981).

3. The unity of the church given in Christ and rooted in the Triune God is realized in our unity in the proclaimed word, the sacraments and the ministry instituted by God and conferred through ordination. It is lived both in the unity of the faith to which we jointly witness, and which together we confess and teach, and in the unity of hope and love which leads us to unite in fully committed fellowship. Unity needs a visible outward form which is able to encompass the element of inner differentiation and spiritual diversity as well as the element of historical change and development. This is the unity of a fellowship which covers all times and places and is summoned to witness and serve the world.[1]

4. It is our conviction that in its essential aspects this view of unity corresponds with the formulation adopted by the Third Assembly of the World Council of Churches at New Delhi in 1961: "We believe that the unity which is both God's will and his gift to his Church is being made visible as all in each place who are baptized into Jesus Christ and confess him as Lord and Saviour are brought by the Holy Spirit into one fully committed fellowship, holding the one apostolic faith, preaching the one Gospel, breaking the one bread, joining in common prayer, and having a corporate life reaching out in witness and service to all and who at the same time are united with the whole Christian fellowship in all places and all ages in such wise that ministry and members are accepted by all, and that all can act and speak together as occasion requires for the tasks to which God calls his people."[2]

---

[1] *Ways to Community,* Roman Catholic/Lutheran Joint Commission, Geneva, 1981, especially Nos. 4–52.

[2] *The New Delhi Report,* London, 1962, Report of Section III, No. 2, p. 116.

a. THE CHURCH AS FELLOWSHIP

5. The one church of Jesus Christ assumes concrete form in local churches which participate in the diversity of historical, cultural and racial situations in which the people live to whom the gospel is proclaimed in word and sacrament. The church is therefore a communion (*communio*) subsisting in a network of local churches. "This Church of Christ is truly present in all legitimate local congregations of the faithful which, united with their pastors, are themselves called churches in the New Testament. For in their own locality these are the new people called by God, in the Holy Spirit and in much fullness (cf. 1 Th. 1:5). In them the faithful are gathered together by the preaching of the gospel of Christ, and the mystery of the Lord's Supper is celebrated... In these communities, though frequently small and poor, or living far from any other, Christ is present. By virtue of Him the one, holy, catholic and apostolic Church gathers together."[3]

6. This view of church unity as communion (*communio*) goes back to the early days of Christianity. It is determinative for the Early Church as well as for the life and ecclesiology of the Orthodox churches. In recent times it has been particularly stressed in Catholic ecclesiology. Part of the fundamental stress of the Second Vatican Council is that the one church exists in and consists of particular churches.[4] "By divine Providence it has come about that various churches established in diverse places by the apostles and their successors have in the course of time coalesced into several groups, organically united, which, preserving the unity of faith and the unique divine constitution of the universal Church, enjoy their own discipline, their own liturgical usage, and their own theological and spiritual heritage... This variety of local churches with one common aspiration is particularly splendid evidence of the catholicity of the undivided Church."[5] This view is regarded as both giving rise to and determining the re-establishment of unity. "The deepening ... of an ecclesiology of communion is ... perhaps the greatest possibility for tomorrow's ecumenism... So far as the reintegration of the Churches into unity is concerned, we have to follow the line of this ecclesiology, which ... is both very ancient and yet very modern."[6]

---

[3] Vatican II, Dogmatic Constitution on the Church, No. 26.
[4] Ibid., No. 23; cf. Codex Iuris Cononici can. 368f.
[5] Vatican II, Dogmatic Constitution on the Church, No. 23.
[6] J. Willebrands, "The Future of Ecumenism", in *One in Christ*, 1975, 4, p. 323.

7. This view of the church and of ecclesial unity is also in accord with Lutheran ecclesiology.[7] The local communities gathered around word and sacrament do not remain isolated as visible forms of the church of Jesus Christ, but rather live in such larger and organically united communities as regional churches, national churches, folk churches, etc. The worldwide Lutheran community, which has the Lutheran World Federation as an instrument, is made up of churches that are bound together by a common understanding of the gospel and by participation in the sacraments which that includes.

b. MODELS OF PARTIAL UNION

8. On the basis of our understanding of the nature of unity, those models appear inadequate which are determined only by concepts of church unity which are only partial. In the opinion of some, however, they can play an important transitional role in certain situations if they are understood either as "steps" on the way to unity or as "partial" expressions of unity; moreover, they can also draw attention to important components of unity.

9. (1) For instance, one can wish to achieve mere *"spiritual" unity* by deliberately dispensing with common ecclesial structures and visible organization. Since the visible manifestations of unity — understood as an essentially spiritual, inward possession — are not expected until the end of time, external features and structures are considered not only superfluous but even as false and harmful. Although such a posture may well remind us of the essential and irrevocable spiritual dimension of all ecumenical efforts,[8] and also of the provisional nature of our expressions of church unity, it nevertheless fails to see the essential visible character of the church and of its unity to such an extent that it cannot be considered as a valid model of unity.

10. (2) This also applies when the unity of the church is expressed in the form of a mere *fellowship-in-dialogue,* where formerly separate communities, delimited and mutually condemnatory, engaged in lively questioning of each other, in listening and speaking. Although dialogue is an essential phase in efforts toward church unity, and although the dialogue

---

[7] Cf. W. Elert, *Abendmahl und Kirchengemeinschaft in der alten Kirche hauptsächlich des Ostens,* Berlin, 1954; Koinonia – Arbeiten des Ökumenischen Ausschusses der Vereinigten Evangelisch-Lutherischen Kirche Deutschlands zur Frage der Kirchen- und Abendmahlsgemeinschaft, Berlin, 1957.
[8] Vatican II, Decree on Ecumenism, No. 8.

momentum must not disappear even in a united church, a mere fellowship-in-dialogue falls short of being a full expression of church unity.

11. (3) Furthermore a form of union which understands itself essentially as *fellowship-of-action* takes seriously the element of common service that is indispensable for a Christian concept of unity, but at the same time (measured by the understanding of unity in No. 3 above) lacks certain essential elements that do not permit it to be seen as a fully valid model of unity. This is true not only of ad hoc fellowship-of-action, but also of such structured church unions as Christian "councils" or "study groups", and church "federations" or "alliances", whose purpose is primarily to facilitate practical cooperation.

12. (4) The practice of *intercommunion* or the proffering of eucharistic hospitality between divided churches must also be seen as only a partial way of expressing unity. The ecumenical and pastoral value of intercommunion or eucharistic hospitality is assessed differently. Some people see in them a step on the way to unity, others regard them as a problematical attempt to realize unity. But it is clear to all that, at the very most, we are here concerned with a provisional expression of unity that will be endangered time and time again, and that it is essential to go further.

c. MODELS OF COMPREHENSIVE UNION

13. In recent ecumenical discussions a series of models of union has been developed and partly practised in the life of the churches. These models correspond more closely to our understanding of unity than the ones mentioned above. They go beyond partial aspects and bring the whole of unity into view. Endeavours to give concrete shape to Catholic-Lutheran church fellowship cannot ignore such discussion and experiences; they are fulfilled in the framework of these discussions, codetermined by them and can receive from them important directives and impulses. Below we describe and briefly analyse the most important and best known of these models. The order in which they are here treated follows an historical rather than systematic sequence.

14. A description of these models must allow for a particular difficulty. Although individual models can be clearly distinguished from each other or can be related to each other, there is often considerable confusion on the level of terminology. This confusion is partly because in some cases a different meaning may be given to the model than is inherent in it. This can be noted, for example, in the case of the model of "conciliar fellowship" and the model of "church fellowship". Therefore, when giving a detailed account of each particular model one should seek to avoid private interpretations. One should always refer to those texts which may

be regarded as the most original, representative or official in character (for example, reports of the Commission on Faith and Order of the World Council of Churches, the Conference of Secretaries of Christian World Communions, the Assemblies of the World Council of Churches, or individual Christian World Communions).

15. The terminological confusion, however, has sometimes found its way even into these more representative texts — for example, concepts of "organic union" or "organic unity" and "corporate fellowship". In each particular instance one should explain how the same concept can refer to differing realities. It helps to clarify the situation and the concepts if a sketch — at least in outline — is given of the motivation and context which have contributed to the development of a model.

1. Organic Union

16. The concept "organic union" or "organic unity" is one of the oldest ecumenical concepts, and it can refer either to a specific understanding of unity or to a particular model of union. The concept which refers to the unity of the church as the "body of Christ" was taken over by the church union movements at the beginning of the century in order to describe their ecumenical goal. In the course of time it received a specific meaning that it had not had originally and, as far as many are concerned, still does not yet have (see also Nos. 19–22 below).

17. According to this specific meaning — which has become increasingly common in the terminology of the Faith and Order movement and then in the World Council of Churches — the model of "organic union" reflects a thinking which regards the existence of different confessional churches as a decisive obstacle to attaining true Christian unity and therefore takes the view that unity can be realized only by surrendering traditional ecclesial and confessional allegiance and identity. "Organic union", which generally comprises the working out of a common confession of faith, agreement about sacraments and ministry, and a homogeneous organizational structure, therefore arises out of the union of existing churches and ecclesial identities to form a "new fellowship with its own new name" and an "identity of its own".[9] It is "costly" and involves "surrender of the denominational identities" through merging "to form one body", "a kind of death" of the denominations which

---

[9] "Concepts of Unity and Models of Union", A Preliminary Study Document of the Faith and Order Commission, October 1972; FO/72:20, IIId and IVb.

existed before; but it is nevertheless regarded as the way "to receive a fuller life".[10]

18. The use of this model of "organic union" has hitherto been concentrated mainly on the local, national and regional levels.

2. Corporate Union

19. Like the concept of "organic union" or "organic unity", the concept of "corporate union" has a long history. In addition, both concepts seem to have been at first identical in content and therefore interchangeable,[11] and indeed many today still regard them as such. At any rate, one must take care to note that "corporate" or "organic" unity or union do not mean here the same thing as the concept of "organic union" in the sense just described (cf. Nos. 16–18 above). The danger here of terminological confusion and factual misunderstanding is particularly great.

20. The concept "corporate union" and the corresponding concept "organic union" confront us, inter alia, in Catholic theologians and the Anglican-Catholic dialogue. There they precisely do not mean realizing unity by surrendering existing ecclesial tradition. Rather, different church communities form in "corporate union" — on the basis of an essential consensus on questions of faith and a joint episcopal constitution as in the Early Church — a fellowship of faith and life in which they as relatively independent corporate members retain a permanent place. They have thereby the possibility and the duty of preserving what in view of the apostolic witness they consider to be of permanent value in their theology and piety placing it in the service of the fellowship as a whole.

21. A merger or mutual absorption of existing ecclesial traditions is rejected because "every church fellowship would lose its character in a fusion of this kind".[12] "Corporate union" is therefore "union in diversity"[13] or, as is said, a unity of churches "which remain churches and nevertheless become one church".[14]

---

[10] *Breaking Barriers,* Nairobi 1975, London/Grand Rapids, 1976, Report of Section II, pp. 65 and 63, Nos. 14 and 10.
[11] *The Second World Conference on Faith and Order,* Edinburgh 1937, London, 1938, pp. 252f.
[12] H. Tenhumberg, "Kirchliche Union bzw. korporative Wiedervereinigung" in *Kirche und Gemeinde,* ed. W. Danielsmeyer and C.H. Ratschow, Witten, 1974, pp. 24f.
[13] J. Ratzinger, Theologische Prinzipienlehre. Bausteine zur Fundamentaltheologie, München, 1981, p. 121.
[14] J. Ratzinger, "Die Kirche und die Kirchen" in *Reformatio,* 1964, p. 105.

22. This model of "corporate union" has now become the declared aim of the Anglican-Catholic dialogue, though with the label "organic unity".[15] In this sense Paul VI, in an address on the occasion of the visit of the Archbishop of Canterbury and referring to the Anglican-Catholic conversations at Malines, said, "The pace of this movement (Anglican-Catholic rapprochement) has quickened marvellously in recent years, so that these words of hope 'The Anglican Church united not absorbed' are no longer a mere dream".[16]

3. Church Fellowship Through Agreement (Concord)

23. A model of union has been developed and become operative among the Lutheran, Reformed and United churches in Europe which is described as "church fellowship". Substantially it is based on a doctrinal agreement (the "Leuenberg Agreement", 1973) jointly drawn up and ratified by these churches.

24. In this context church fellowship means: "On the basis of the consensus they have reached in their understanding of the gospel" and on the basis of having determined that "the doctrinal condemnations expressed in the confessional documents no longer apply to the contemporary doctrinal position of the assenting churches", the various churches accord each other "fellowship in Word and sacrament" ("table and pulpit fellowship") and also fellowship in the ecclesial ministry ("mutual recognition of ordination and the freedom to provide for intercelebration").[17] The doctrinal agreement here involved does not imply a "new confession of faith".[18] Rather, the church fellowship made possible by this agreement is a fellowship among "churches with different confessional positions" in continuing "loyalty to the confessions of faith which bind them, or with due respect for their traditions".[19]

25. Although such a church fellowship understands itself as the realization of church unity in the full sense, it does not consider itself as something sealed and static. Rather, it contains a dynamic element in as much as the churches constituting the fellowship pledge themselves to

---

[15] Final Report of the Anglican-Roman Catholic International Commission, 1981, Conclusion, in *Growth in Agreement,* Reports and Agreed Statements of Ecumenial Conversations on a World Level, edited by Harding Meyer and Lukas Vischer, New York/Geneva, 1984, p. 116.
[16] Acta Apostolicae Sedis, 1977, No. 5, p. 284.
[17] Leuenberg Agreement, Nos 29–33.
[18] Ibid., No. 37.
[19] Ibid., Nos. 29 and 30.

"strive for the fullest possible cooperation in witness and service to the world".[20] Furthermore, this orientation towards a continual confirmation and deepening of the fellowship is expressed in the fact that the churches "pledge themselves to their common doctrinal discussions".[21]

26. Although this model of a church fellowship through agreement (concord) was first developed and practised in the context of the Lutheran, Reformed and United churches in Europe, it is fundamentally open and applicable also to other churches and other geographical regions. Indeed it is no longer limited to Europe.

4. Conciliar Fellowship

27. By taking up and purposely elaborating the statements made at New Delhi and Uppsala, the Commission on Faith and Order developed the concept of "conciliar fellowship" which was received by the WCC Assembly in Nairobi, 1975. Although "conciliar fellowship" can also "refer to a quality of life within each local church",[22] in the true sense this concept denotes a detailed model of union.

28. This "conciliar fellowship" model finds its application not so much at the level of the local churches but "in the first place it expresses the unity of church separated by distance, culture and time".[23] It intends to be, therefore, a model of union on a wider level, ultimately on the level of the universal church. The definition says: "The one Church is to be envisioned as a conciliar fellowship of local churches which are themselves truly united."[24]

29. In this "conciliar fellowship" the various local churches "recognize the others as belonging to the same Church of Christ", confess the same apostolic faith, have full communion with one another in baptism and eucharist, recognize each other's members and ministries, and are one in witness and service in and before the world. The structural bond necessary for the "conciliar fellowship" is provided primarily by "conciliar gatherings",[25] i.e., by means of "representative gatherings".[26] Both Cath-

---

[20] Ibid., No. 29.
[21] Ibid., No. 37.
[22] Nairobi, op. cit., p. 60, No. 4.
[23] Ibid.
[24] Ibid., No. 3; cf. the definition of "local church", "The Unity of the Church — Next Steps", in *What Kind of Unity?* Faith and Order Paper 69, Geneva, 1974, p. 123.
[25] Nairobi, op. cit., p. 60, No. 3.
[26] "The Unity of the Church — Next Steps", op. cit., A.III.3, p. 122.

olics and Orthodox stress thereby that "conciliar fellowship" necessarily encompasses also the ministry transmitted in apostolic succession.

30. "Conciliar fellowship" does not mean a monolithic unity,[27] but rather a "diversity" which must "not only be admitted but actively desired".[28] For a long time it was not at all clear what place amid these diversities would be accorded the individual church or confessional traditions, especially since the "conciliar fellowship" model seemed to be very closely connected with the model of "organic union" (see Nos. 16–18 above).[29] Indeed, it seemed to presuppose "organic union".[30] In the meantime these considerations have been further developed by the Commission on Faith and Order[31] and also by other bodies[32] in such a way that confessional traditions can undoubtedly retain an identifiable life in this "conciliar fellowship", provided that this will not call into question the basic elements of "conciliar fellowship".

5. Unity in Reconciled Diversity

31. There have always been tendencies within the ecumenical movement that aimed at an ecumenical fellowship in which the existing ecclesial traditions with their particularity and diversity would remain in integrity and authenticity. The above described models of "corporate union" (see Nos. 19–22 above) and of "church fellowship by means of agreement" (see Nos. 23–26 above) are examples of this.

32. In this sense, and against the background of intensified ecumenical commitment on the part of the churches and Christian World Communions, the model of "unity in reconciled diversity" has recently been developed.[33] It is based on the idea that "the variety of denominational

---

[27] Nairobi, op. cit., p. 60, No. 4.
[28] Ibid., p. 61, No. 7.
[29] "The Unity of the Church — Next Steps", op. cit., A.IV, pp. 123ff.
[30] Accra Report, "The Unity of the Church: The Goal and the Way", in *Uniting in Hope*, Accra 1974, Faith and Order Paper No. 72, p. 114.
[31] *Sharing in One Hope*, Commission on Faith and Order, Bangalore 1978, Faith and Order Paper No. 92, Geneva, pp. 235–242.
[32] For example at the First Forum on Bilateral Conversations April 1978 or at the Consultation between the World Council of Churches and the World Confessional Families (Geneva, October 1978), see *LWF Report*, No. 15, June 1983, Günther Gassmann/Harding Meyer, "The Unity of the Church — Requirements and Structure", pp. 33–39, 50–54.
[33] "The Ecumenical Role of the World Confessional Families in the One Ecumenical Movement", discussion paper from two consultations with representatives from world confessional families, Geneva 1974, Nos. 17–21, *LWF Report*, No. 15, June 1983, pp. 27f.

heritages (is) legitimate" and forms part of "the richness of life in the church universal". When "in the open encounter with other heritages" the existing traditions and denominations lose their "exclusive" and "divisive character, there emerges a vision of unity that has the character of a 'reconciled diversity' ".[34]

33. The idea of "unity in reconciled diversity" means that "expression would be given to the abiding value of the confessional forms of the Christian faith in all their variety" and that these diversities, "when related to the central message of salvation and Christian faith" and when they "ring out, (are) transformed and renewed" in the process of ecumenical encounter and theological dialogue, they "lose their divisive character and are reconciled to each other ... into a binding ecumenical fellowship in which even the confessional elements" are preserved.[35] Unity in "reconciled diversity" therefore does not mean "mere coexistence". It means "genuine church fellowship, including as essential elements the recognition of baptism, the establishing of eucharistic fellowship, the mutual recognition of church ministries, and a binding common purpose of witness and service".[36]

34. The model of "unity in reconciled diversity" comes "very close to the concept of 'conciliar fellowship' ... and cannot be put forward as a rival to this concept". The tension felt occasionally in the beginning vis-à-vis the model of "conciliar fellowship" — "that the latter seems to take insufficiently into account the legitimacy of the confessional differences and therefore the need to preserve them",[37] — seems to have been largely overcome in the meantime.[38]

d. THE EXAMPLE OF THE UNION OF FLORENCE

35. For possible church union without merger or absorption, the example of Florence is important.

---

[34] Ibid., No. 30, p. 31.
[35] *In Christ — A New Community*, The Proceedings of the Sixth Assembly of the Lutheran World Federation, Dar-es-Salaam 1977, Geneva, 1977, Statement on Models of Unity, p. 174.
[36] Ibid., p. 174; cf. *Ecumenical Relations of the Lutheran World Federation*, Report of the Working Group on the Interrelations Between the Various Bilateral Dialogues, Geneva, 1977, No. 154.
[37] *In Christ — A New Community*, op. cit., p. 174.
[38] See above, No. 30; cf. G. Gassmann/H. Meyer, "The Unity of the Church", op. cit., pp. 15ff.

36. The union between the Latin and Byzantine churches formed at the Council of Florence did not represent a merger. Without prejudicing the unity of faith basic to the fellowship, each church preserved its own liturgical, canonical and theological tradition. This common faith could be expressed in various formulations (for example, as regards the "procession" of the Holy Spirit) and tolerate diversities of discipline (for example the toleration of remarriage of divorced Christians of the Greek but not of the Latin rites, a differentiation still operative at Trent).

37. Even though this attempt failed, impulses from Florence did not remain without effect. It is due to them that the Roman Catholic Church can no longer be identified by its Latinism. Following Vatican II, however, the model of sister churches applies, a model that is inspired by the relationships that existed during the first millennium.[39]

38. Moreover, several statements made by Vatican II about the united Eastern churches are of great importance in the search for a model of unity in diversity. There we read: "That Church, Holy and Catholic, which is the Mystical Body of Christ, is made up of the faithful who are organically united in the Holy Spirit through the same faith, the same sacraments, and the same government and who, combining into various groups held together by a hierarchy, form separate Churches or rites."[40] "Such individual Churches, whether of the East or of the West ... differ somewhat among themselves in what are called rites (that is, in liturgy, ecclesiastical discipline and spiritual heritage) ..."[41] "Therefore, attention should everywhere be given to the preservation and growth of each individual Church. For this purpose, parishes and a special hierarchy should be established for each where the spiritual good of the faithful so demands. The Ordinaries of the various individual Churches which have jurisdiction in the same territory should, by taking common counsel in regular meetings, strive to promote unity of action."[42]

39. Vatican II, therefore, does not call for a single jurisdiction or a single bishop in each particular case. Moreover, the Council considers it to be legitimate for the church of one particular rite, i.e., a church with its own spiritual, theological and canonical tradition, to reach out everywhere, even beyond its original geographical limits. Admittedly, it is a question here of provisional measures in the expectation of the restoration of unity

---

[39] Tomos Agapis. Dokumentation zum Dialog der Liebe zwischen dem Hl. Stuhl und dem Ökumenischen Patriarchat 1958–1976, edited on behalf of the Stiftungs-fonds PRO ORIENTE, Vienna. Innsbruck, Vienna, Munich, 1978, passim.
[40] Vatican II, Decree on Eastern Catholic Churches, No. 2.
[41] Ibid., No. 3.
[42] Ibid., No. 4.

between the Roman Catholic Church and the Eastern churches which are not yet in full fellowship with it.[43]

40. The example of Florence shows that it is possible for the Roman Catholic Church to unite with another church without merger if that church confesses the same faith and if the mutual recognition of ministries can be achieved. For this example shows

— the possibility, at least temporarily, of the presence of two bishops at the same place and

— the justification of different theological, canonical and spiritual traditions carried by these different episcopal jurisdictions.

e. FELLOWSHIP OF SISTER CHURCHES

41. Without being able to refer to them as "models" of union in the strict sense, two concepts merit particular attention, which have proved to be important and useful in endeavours to conceive of and practise models of union. Both concepts, each in its own way, express and underscore the idea of unity in diversity as emphasized particularly by some of the models of union described above ("corporate union", see Nos. 19–22 above; "church fellowship through agreement", see Nos. 23–26 above).

1. Ecclesial "Types"

42. The view was taken repeatedly in the past that the ecumenical problem derives from the fact that, ever since the early days, distinct basic types and archetypes of the faith have existed within Christianity; these types, though fundamentally interconnected, differ distinctively from each other with regard to specific characteristics of piety, doctrine, ethos, ecclesial structures, etc. and manifest themselves, to some extent, in the existing churches. The ecumenical task, then, would not consist of eliminating these different basic types or of merging them, but rather of making visible their legitimacy and of preserving and keeping them together in the fellowship of the one church for which we strive.

43. The view that within Christianity there exist different ecclesial types (*typoi*) has also been presented in more recent times. The term "typos", for example, has been defined as follows: "Where there is a long coherent tradition, commanding men's love and loyalty, creating and sustaining

---

[43] Cf. ibid., No. 30.

a harmonious and organic whole of complementary elements, each of which supports and strengthens the other, you have the reality of a typos." The elements that constitute each ecclesial "typos" are a "characteristic theological method and approach", "a characteristic liturgical expression", a specific "spiritual and devotional tradition", a "characteristic canonical discipline". "The life of the Church needs a variety of *typoi* which would manifest the full catholic and apostolic character of the one and holy Church."[44]

2. Sister Churches

44. Recently the concept of "sister churches" has become even more important. As an expression of the fellowship between individual local churches it has a long tradition that goes right back to the Early Church and was used in this sense by the Second Vatican Council.[45] For some time this concept has also been used to describe fellowship that has been regained or aspired to between separated churches, especially in the ecumenical relations between the Roman Catholic Church and the Orthodox churches.

45. This new usage goes back above all to the message that Pope Paul VI sent to the Ecumenical Patriarch Athenagoras I. It reads as follows: "Now, after a long period of division and reciprocal incomprehension the Lord grants us that we rediscover ourselves as sister churches despite the obstacles which were then raised between us. In the light of Christ, we see how urgent is the necessity of surmounting these obstacles in order to succeed in bringing to its fullness and perfection that unity — already so rich — which exists between us." This fellowship between "sister churches" is a fellowship in diversity. "It is a matter of knowing and of respecting each other in the legitimate diversity of liturgical, spiritual, disciplinary and theological traditions (cf. council's Decree on Ecumenism, Nos. 14 and 17) by means of a frank theological dialogue, made possible by the re-establishment of brotherly charity in order to attain accord in the sincere confession of all revealed truths."[46]

---

[44] Jan Cardinal Willebrands, in an address given to representatives of the Anglican Communion in Cambridge, England, January 1970; text published in *Documents on Anglican-Roman Catholic Relations,* Washington, 1972, pp. 39ff.
[45] Vatican II, Decree on Ecumenism, No. 14.
[46] Message of Pope Paul VI to Patriarch Athenagoras I on July 25, 1967. Information Service, The Secretariat for Promoting Christian Unity, 1967/3, pp. 12f; AAS 59, 1967, pp. 852–854.

Part II

Forms and Phases of Catholic-Lutheran Fellowship

ON THE WAY TO CHURCH FELLOWSHIP

46. All the models of union described above undoubtedly contain valuable pointers for shaping Catholic-Lutheran church fellowship. Nevertheless, none of these models was worked out in a specifically Catholic-Lutheran context. One must therefore ask whether, in envisioning a promising form of Catholic-Lutheran fellowship, one should not consider more closely the particularities of that relationship. One should by no means assume, however, that there exists one single model which can lead us to fellowship.

47. What is significant and useful in the foregoing description and analysis of the various models of union for the shaping of the Catholic-Lutheran fellowship is: The unity we seek will be a unity in diversity. Particularities developed within the two traditions will not merely be fused, nor their differences completely given up.

This is underscored by the models of "unity in reconciled diversity", "corporate union", "church fellowship through agreement" as well as by the concepts of "typos" and "sister churches".

What is really at stake is that a theologically based agreement of the type that already exists in the Catholic-Lutheran dialogue should work through divergences to the point where they lose their church divisive character. At the same time it should both clarify and make certain that remaining differences are based on a fundamental consensus in understanding the apostolic faith and therefore are legitimate.

This aspect is particularly stressed by the models of "unity in reconciled diversity" and "church fellowship through agreement".

Once the divergences of both traditions have lost their divisive force, they can no longer be the subject of mutual condemnation. It should be publicly declared that they are now groundless.

This is emphasized, above all, by the model of "church fellowship through agreement".

The unity we seek must be rooted in common sacramental life.

This is implied by all models, but is particularly implicit in the understanding of unity as *communio*.

The unity we seek must assume concrete form in suitable structures that would enable our hitherto separated communities to lead a truly common life and to make joint action possible both at the level of the local churches and at the universal level.

This is stressed particularly by the models of "organic union" and "conciliar fellowship".

In our endeavours to find the appropriate structures needed for full and binding fellowship we shall have to face up to the question of jointly exercising the ministry of church leadership, present in the office of bishop in the Early Church.

This is one of the presuppositions of the model of "corporate union".

48. Christian reconciliation plays an important part in all the forms and phases of the unity we seek. We jointly confess that we have been reconciled with God through Christ. As we acknowledge this with thanksgiving and praise, we must also confess our sins and errors and know ourselves to be called to be reconciled with others.

The mutual reconciliation which we seek as Christians of different churches and which stands entirely under the reconciliation that occurred in Christ, does not simply eliminate our differences. There are differences that stem from error and weakness of faith and which cannot therefore be overcome without repentance, self-criticism and renewal. Here reconciliation has its price. But there are also differences between us that derive from the fact that the one church of Christ exists in various places and that one and the same faith can be expressed and lived in different ways. We can recognize such differences as legitimate, yes even accept them with joy as far as they enable us to learn from each other, correct, stimulate or enrich us.

This mutual recognition, which can be achieved step by step, is decisive for the process of reconciliation. Reconciliation cannot happen without the freedom, given us through Christ's reconciliation, from our instinctive fear of the other as stranger and our anxious concern for our own identity.

Reconciliation is not possible without dialogue and constant communication. It is a process of discerning the spirits and of searching for steps along a pathway known only to God. Reconciliation is thus a dynamic process, even where church unity exists or has been re-established. For as long as sin and conflict remain and as long as Christians and churches live in changing times and in a diverse world, this process will not be completed.

49. The dynamic inherent in the process of reconciliation and the realizing of church fellowship unfolds itself more clearly in the efforts for

a. fellowship in confessing the one apostolic faith (community of faith),

b. fellowship in sacramental life (community in sacraments)

c. fellowship as a structured fellowship in which community of faith and community in sacraments find adequate ecclesial form and in which common life, common decisions and common action are not only possible; they are required (community of service).

During this process of realizing church fellowship there is no sequential or gradational relationship between the achievement of community of faith, community in sacraments, and community of service. According to our understanding of unity (see No. 3 above) the concretization of church fellowship rather constitutes an integral process in which each of these three elements achieves full realization only together with the others. This process is characterized by the two interrelated aims of "recognition" and "reception".[47]

---

[47] The two concepts must be distinguished from each other. Each of them has a distinct meaning and conceptual history. Cf. in the vast literature for example: A. Grillmeier, "Konzil und Rezeption. Methodische Bemerkungen zu einem Thema der ökumenischen Diskussion der Gegenwart", *Theologie und Philosophie* 45, 1970, pp. 321–352; Y. Congar, "La 'réception' comme réalité ecclésiologique", *Revue des Sciences Philosophiques et Théologiques* 56, 1972, pp. 369–403; G. Gassmann, "Rezeption im ökumenischen Kontext", *Ökumenische Rundschau* 26, 1977, pp. 314–327; H. Meyer, " 'Anerkennung' – Ein ökumenischer Schlüsselbegriff", Dialog und Anerkennung. Beiheft zur Ökumenischen Rundschau No. 37, Frankfurt, 1978, pp. 25–41; M. Garijo, "Der Begriff der 'Rezeption' und sein Ort im Kern der katholischen Ekklesiologie", *Theologischer Konsens und Kirchenspaltung*, edited by P. Lengsfeld and H.G. Stobbe, Stuttgart, 1981, pp. 97–109, and Anmerkungen, pp. 167–172; E. Lanne, "La 'réception' ", *Irénikon* vol. LV, 1982, pp. 199–213.

The term "reception" is often used with regard to accepting specific statements or documents, but here we intend both terms, "reception" and "recognition", to be designations of interchurch relations and actions:

"Recognition" means basically a theological and spiritual affirmation of the other church in its special emphases, which confers on this church — as a whole or in individual elements of its belief, life or structure — legitimacy and authenticity.

"Reception" means basically a theological and spiritual affirmation of the other church — as a whole or in individual elements of its belief, life or structure — which accepts and appropriates the special emphases of the other church either as its own or as contributions (in the sense of correction or complement). ▶

50. The stage of full mutual recognition has not yet been attained between our churches, although it is beginning to reveal itself.

In recent years a broad process of comprehension and rapprochement embracing all levels of church life has led to the fact that our churches see each other in a completely different way than before. Likewise, recent decades have seen positive changes with regard to forms of thought and life of our churches which shaped them and greatly influenced their relationship with each other.

51. True to the spirit of Vatican II (see No. 53 below), the Roman Catholic Church has changed its view vis-à-vis the Lutheran churches. A reassessment both of the common past and of the Lutheran heritage has taken place. This is clearly expressed by the words of Pope John Paul II on the occasion of his visit to the land of Luther in 1980.

With regard to the history of our separation the Pope said: " 'Let us no more pass judgment on one another' (Rom 14:13). Let us rather recognize our guilt. 'All have sinned' (Rom 3:23) applies also with regard to the grace of unity. We must see and say this in all earnestness and draw our conclusions from it." "If we do not evade the facts we realize that the faults of men led to the unhappy division of Christians, and that our faults again hinder the possible and necessary steps towards unity. I emphatically make my own what my predecessor Hadrian VI said in 1523 at the Diet of Nuremberg: 'Certainly the Lord's hand has not been shortened so much that he cannot save us, but sin separates us from him. ... All of us, prelates and priests, have strayed from the right path and there is not anyone who does good (cf. Ps 14:3). Therefore must all render honour to God and humble ourselves before him. Each of us must

---

Therefore "recognition" and "reception" each involve a specific emphasis: "Recognition" stresses more strongly the special character of the other in its independence, an independence capable of fellowship. "Reception" emphasizes more strongly the special character of the other as containing elements to be adopted and integrated into a church's own life and thinking and into its fellowship with the other church. "Recognition" and "reception" must go hand in hand and complement each other in efforts for church fellowship. There can be no "reception" without recognition of the legitimacy and authenticity of the other. "Recognition" calls for beginning the process of accepting and adopting the particular features of the other in as much as they represent a contribution to the life and thinking of the partner and are considered as necessary for realizing the fellowship.

consider why he has fallen and judge himself rather than be judged by God on the day of wrath.' "[48]

On the occasion of Martin Luther's 500th anniversary the Pope wrote: "In fact, the scientific researches of Evangelical and Catholic scholars, researches whose results have already reached notable points of convergence, have led to the delineation of a more complete and more differentiated picture of Luther's personality and of the complex texture of the social, political and ecclesial historical realities of the first half of the sixteenth century. Consequently there is clearly outlined the deep religious feeling of Luther who was driven with burning passion by the question of eternal salvation."[49]

Concerning the Catholic-Lutheran dialogue, particularly the conversation on the Augsburg Confession, the Pope took up the statement of the German Catholic bishops: "Let us rejoice to discover not only partial consent on some truths, but also agreement on the fundamental and central truths. That lets us hope for unity also in the areas of our faith and our life in which we are still divided up to now."[50]

52. In the Lutheran churches, likewise, there has been a profound change of attitude vis-à-vis the Catholic Church. With reference to the plea for forgiveness of Pope Paul VI and in answer to it, the Fifth LWF Assembly (1970) stated: "It is ... in accordance with this commandment of truth and love that we as Lutheran Christians and congregations be prepared to acknowledge that the judgment of the Reformers upon the Roman Catholic Church and its theology was not entirely free of polemical distortions, which in part have been perpetuated to the present day. We are truly sorry for the offense and misunderstanding which these polemic elements have caused our Roman Catholic brethren. We remember with gratitude the statement of Pope Paul VI to the Second Vatican Council in which he communicates his plea for forgiveness for any offense caused by the Roman Catholic Church. ... Together with all Christians (we) pray for forgiveness in the prayer our Lord has taught us."[51]

---

[48] Pope John Paul II in Germany. Information Service, The Secretariat for Promoting Christian Unity, No. 45, 1981/I, pp. 5f.; p. 7.
[49] Pope John Paul II's Letter on Fifth Centenary of Birth of Martin Luther to Cardinal Willebrands, President of the Secretariat for Promoting Christian Unity. Information Service, op. cit., No. 52, 1983/III, p. 83.
[50] Pope John Paul II in Germany. Information Service, op. cit., No. 45, 1981/I, p. 6.; cf. Pastoral Letter of German Bishops "Thy Kingdom come" (20 January 1980), KNA-Dokumentation No. 5, 23 January 1980; and Lutheran/Roman Catholic Discussion on the Augsburg Confession, Documents 1977–1981, edited by Harding Meyer, LWF Report, No. 10, August 1980, pp. 55 and 64.
[51] Sent Into the World, The Proceedings of the Fifth Assembly of the Lutheran World Federation, Evian 1970, Minneapolis, 1971, pp. 156f.

The presence of official Lutheran observers at all the sessions of the Second Vatican Council, the subsequent beginning of bilateral dialogues both at the world level and in many countries, closer life together and increased cooperation with local Catholic churches, parishes and Catholic Christians have led Lutherans to a new understanding of Catholic piety, church life and teaching. The Roman Catholic Church is no longer regarded as "false church". Many differences have lost their former unfamiliarity and divisive rigour as far as Lutheran sensitivity is concerned. One now encounters a general readiness to abandon long-standing negative prejudices and to examine doctrinal condemnations pronounced in the past to see whether they are still valid today. Thus, for example, the papal office and its holders appear in a new light that makes former condemnations and the hostile images of the past untenable. In view of common theological understandings and liturgical developments in both churches, the sharp condemnation of Catholic Mass is considered to belong to the past, as is shown, for example, by the decisions of some Lutheran churches in favour of reciprocal eucharistic hospitality.[52]

53. The Roman Catholic Church has not only changed its attitude vis-à-vis the Lutheran churches but with Vatican II has also renewed its forms of thought and life.

— Vatican II adopted an understanding of church that does not exclusively identify the Roman Catholic Church with the church of Jesus Christ, but also recognizes the church of Jesus Christ outside its bounds in other churches and ecclesial communities.[53]

— Attention to the " 'hierarchy' of truths", as called for by the Decree on Ecumenism,[54] implies that every theological statement must be

---

[52] Cf. The recommendations regarding eucharistic hospitality by the Church of the Augsburg Confession of Alsace and Lorraine, December 1973, *Lutheran World,* 22, 1975, pp. 152ff; and the "Pastoraltheologische Handreichung der Vereinigten Evangelisch-Lutherischen Kirche Deutschlands" regarding the question of the participation of Lutheran Christians in the celebration of the eucharist by other confessions, 1975. Cf. also *A Statement on Communion Practices,* ALC/ LCA, 1978, p. 7, "Intercommunion".

[53] The affirmations that the Church of Christ "subsists in the Catholic Church" (Vatican II, Dogmatic Constitution on the Church, No. 8) and that the Spirit of Christ has not refrained from using "these separated Churches and Communities ... as means of salvation" (ibid., Decree on Ecumenism, No. 3) show that the Catholic Church does not identify the church of God with its own visible boundaries. This constitutes a considerable change in attitude. It indicates a recognition that "some, even very many, of the most significant elements or endowments which together go to build up and give life to the Church herself can exist outside the visible boundaries of the Catholic Church" (ibid.) and an awareness "that whatever is wrought by the grace of the Holy Spirit in the hearts of our separated brethren can contribute to our own edification" (ibid., No. 4).

[54] Ibid., Decree on Ecumenism, No. 11.

related to the foundation of the Christian faith. Lutherans have similar concerns.[55]

— Moreover, in its forms of piety, its liturgical life (celebration of Mass, for example) and its government (for example by the general development of synodal elements at all levels of church life), the Catholic Church is reflecting on its origins, thereby showing concretely that in each of these areas it understands itself as a church in need of "continual reformation".[56]

54. A renewal of the forms of theological thinking and ecclesial life is also taking place in the Lutheran churches.

— The renewed orientation in the early decades of this century to the Reformation and Reformation theology accompanied by a historical examination of developments in the Early Church and the Middle Ages has led in recent decades to a deepened understanding of church, ecclesial ministry and worship.

— The sacramental dimension of worship preserved during the Reformation but often diminished later, is again emphasized without weakening the stress on the word. In many respects this emphasis has reshaped the liturgical life of the Lutheran churches.

— The normative function of Scripture in the life, teaching and proclamation of the church continues to be maintained; an exclusivistic understanding of Scripture, detached from the transmission process and church tradition, seems to have been overcome.

— Continuity with the Early Church, which was preserved and indeed stressed by the Reformers, is again seen more clearly and is creating an enhanced awareness of the ecumenicity and catholicity of the Lutheran confession.

a. COMMUNITY OF FAITH

55. For Catholics and Lutherans alike the common confession of the one apostolic faith means (1) bearing joint witness to this faith, (2) taking account of legitimate differences, and (3) overcoming the obstacles raised by earlier mutual condemnations.

---

[55] Cf. "The Gospel and the Church" (Malta Report), No. 25.
[56] Vatican II, Decree on Ecumenism, No. 6; cf. also Dogmatic Constitution on the Church, No. 8.

1. Joint Witness to the Apostolic Faith

56. For the unity of our churches and especially for our task of preaching, common witness to the apostolic faith is of fundamental importance. If we apply the principle of the " 'hierarchy' of truths", the christological and trinitarian centre or "foundation of the Christian faith" is primarily at stake.[57] It is from there that the full catholicity of the faith is again to be mutually comprehended. Such an endeavour will bring about shifts of emphasis and changes in the self-understanding of our churches: overcoming of one-sidedness, loosening of constraints, correction of certain exaggerations.

57. This process is already under way:

— The starting point is the common affirmation of the faith of the Early Church, formulated by the early councils in obedience to Holy Scripture and witnessed to in the creeds of the Early Church (Apostles' Creed, Nicene Creed, Athanasian Creed).[58]

> "Together we confess the faith in the Triune God and the saving work of God through Jesus Christ in the Holy Spirit... Through all the disputes and differences of the 16th century, Lutheran and Catholic Christians remained one in this central and most important truth of the Christian faith."[59]

— The process of growth in common witness is advanced by a new consensus regarding the relationship between *Holy Scripture and tradition,* long the subject of controversy:

> "This poses the old controversial question regarding the relationship of Scripture and tradition in a new way. The Scripture can no longer be exclusively contrasted with tradition, because the New Testament itself is the product of primitive tradition. Yet as the witness to the fundamental tradition, Scripture has a normative role for the entire later tradition of the church."[60]

---

[57] Ibid., Decree on Ecumenism, No. 11; cf. Malta Report, Nos. 24f.

[58] Cf. The Book of Concord, The Confessions of the Evangelical Lutheran Church, translated and edited by Theodore G. Tappert, Philadelphia 1979, pp. 17ff.

[59] "All Under One Christ", No. 13; cf. *Lutherans and Catholics in Dialogue* I, "The Status of the Nicene Creed as Dogma of the Church", Washington D.C., 1965; and "Erklärung zur 1600-Jahr-Feier des Glaubensbekenntnisses von Nizäa-Konstantinopel" of the Joint Commission of representatives from the Evangelical Church in Germany and the Catholic Church, *KNA Dokumentation,* No. 16, 3 June 1981.

[60] Malta Report, No. 17.

— It extends to our understanding of the gospel expressed during the Reformation particularly in the *doctrine of justification:*

"Today, however, a far-reaching consensus is developing in the interpretation of justification. Catholic theologians also emphasize in reference to justification that God's gift of salvation for the believer is unconditional as far as human accomplishments are concerned. Lutheran theologians emphasize that the event of justification is not limited to individual forgiveness of sins, and they do not see in it a purely external declaration of the justification of the sinner. Rather the righteousness of God actualized in the Christ event is conveyed to the sinner through the message of justification as an encompassing reality basic to the new life of the believer."[61] "It is solely by grace and by faith in Christ's saving work and not because of any merit in us that we are accepted by God and receive the Holy Spirit who renews our hearts and equips us for and calls us to good works."[62]

— It entails a far-reaching consensus regarding the *understanding and the celebration of the eucharist* (see No. 76 below).[63]

— It has led to a basic though not yet complete consensus in the *understanding of church:*

"By church we mean the communion of those whom God gathers together through Christ in the Holy Spirit, by the proclamation of the gospel and the administration of the sacraments, and the ministry instituted by him for his purpose. Though it always includes sinners, yet in virtue of the promise and fidelity of God it is the one, holy, catholic and apostolic church which is to continue forever."[64] "It stands under the gospel and has the gospel as its superordinate criterion;" ... its "authority ... can only be service of the word and ... it is not master of the word of the Lord."[65]

— It extends also to the *understanding and exercise of the ordained ministry in the church:*

The special ecclesial ministry, which is transmitted by ordination (see No. 71 below), "is instituted by Jesus Christ"[66] and as such

---

[61] Ibid., No. 26.
[62] "All Under One Christ", No. 14.
[63] Cf. *The Eucharist,* Nos. 1–45 and 76; cf. also "The Liturgical Celebration of the Eucharist", ibid., pp. 29ff.
[64] "All Under One Christ", No. 16.
[65] Malta Report, Nos. 48 and 21.
[66] *The Ministry in the Church,* No. 20.

"is constitutive for the church".[67] Its specific function is "to assemble and build up the Christian community by proclaiming the word of God, celebrating the sacraments and presiding over the liturgical, missionary and diaconal life of the community".[68] In performing this function the ministry stands "in the midst of the whole people and for the people of God", but "inasmuch as the ministry is exercised on behalf of Jesus Christ and makes him present, it has authority over against the community".[69]

58. Even though efforts toward consensus regarding the apostolic faith must be continued, as was shown particularly clearly in our common reflection on the Augsburg Confession, one may already say that we can "discover not simply a partial consensus on some truths, but rather a full accord on fundamental and central truths",[70] to put it in the words of Pope John Paul II and of the German Catholic bishops.

59. The Executive Committee of the Lutheran World Federation took this up and announced: "We ... agree that ... Roman Catholics and Lutherans 'have discovered that they have a common mind on basic doctrinal truths which points to Jesus Christ, the living center of our faith' ("All Under One Christ", No. 17) and that therefore with regard to the Augsburg Confession one may and should speak of 'a full accord on fundamental and central truths' ... or respectively of a 'basic consensus' of faith (ibid., paras. 18 and 25)."[71]

60. To reach the goal in this effort towards consensus in the apostolic faith, one must take account of how our two churches understand and practise *doctrinally authoritative teaching,* and which office holders may therefore in the name of our churches pronounce an official judgment about the theological consensus attained in our dialogue.

In the Roman Catholic Church the function of authoritative teaching is in a special manner the task of the bishops, who discharge this task "in a many-sided exchange regarding faith with believers, priests, and theologians".[72] Doctrinal decisions of the church are ultimately binding when "the bishops interpret the revealed faith in universal agreement with each other and in communion with the Bishop of Rome".[73]

---

[67] "All Under One Christ", No. 18; cf. *The Ministry in the Church,* No. 17.
[68] *The Ministry in the Church,* No. 31.
[69] Ibid., Nos. 14 and 23.
[70] See footnote 50 above.
[71] "Lutheran/Roman Catholic Discussion on the Augsburg Confession Documents 1977–1981", op. cit. p. 76.
[72] *The Ministry in the Church,* No. 51.
[73] Ibid., No. 52.

In the Lutheran interpretation, too, "the holders of the episcopal office are ... entrusted in a special manner with the task of watching over the purity of the gospel".[74] But in most Lutheran churches authoritative teaching is effected more in a process of consensus-building in which church leaders or bishops, teachers of theology, pastors and non-ordained members of the congregation participate with basically equal rights. Usually this process has synodal forms.[75]

Authoritative teaching in both churches is subject to the norm of the gospel[76] and is oriented to past doctrinal decisions recognized as binding. In both churches doctrinal decisions, if they are to become fruitful and develop their full situational force, depend on far-reaching reception in the consciousness and life of the local churches, congregations and believers.[77]

It can therefore be seen that both churches can and do teach in an authoritative way and that in spite of existing differences, there are important parallels in achieving authoritative teaching. Thus, it is possible for both churches, each in its own way, to accord authoritative character to the agreements in their understanding of the apostolic faith which they have attained. It would be important to ensure that this process, going on within the two churches, even now proceeds with a certain degree of synchronization and as much commonality as possible.

2. Unity of Faith in the Diversity of its Forms of Expression

61.   Unity in the same faith does not mean uniformity in the way it is articulated and expressed. This is one of the basic presuppositions of the ecumenical movement of our century.[78]

Whenever the reference is to doctrine and life, Reformation theology reiterates the conviction that complete conformity is not a condition for church unity.[79]

---

[74] Ibid., No. 53.
[75] Cf. ibid., No. 55.
[76] Ibid., No. 57.
[77] Cf. ibid., Nos. 52 and 54.
[78] Already during the first World Conference on Faith and Order it was said that "unity ... does not mean uniformity". Reports of the World Conference on Faith and Order, Lausanne, August 1927, Boston, 1928, Report on Subject VII, p. 20.
[79] Augsburg Confession, VII, The Book of Concord, p. 32; cf. Luther's comment to the confession of the Bohemian Brethren, WA 50, p. 380; Confessio Helvetica Posterior, XVII; 39 Articles, Art. 19.

62. Vatican II states: "While preserving unity in essentials, let all members of the Church, according to the office entrusted to each, preserve a proper freedom in the various forms of spiritual life and discipline, in the variety of liturgical rites, and even in the theological elaborations of revealed truths."[80]

In this sense Pope Paul VI expressed himself repeatedly and, in doing so, gave even more concrete shape to the idea of unity of faith in the diversity of its forms of expression. In his speech in the Cathedral of Phanar (1967) he said: "In the light of our love for Christ and of our brotherly love, we perceive even more clearly the profound identity of our faith, and the points on which we still differ must not prevent us from seeing this profound unity. And here, too, charity must come to our aid, as it helped Hilary and Athanasius to recognize the sameness of the faith underlying the differences of vocabulary at a time when serious disagreements were creating divisions among Christian bishops. Did not pastoral love prompt St. Basil, in his defense of the true faith in the Holy Spirit, to refrain from using certain terms which, accurate though they were, could have given rise to scandal in one part of the Christian people? And did not St. Cyril of Alexandria consent in 433 to abandon his beautiful formulation of theology in the interest of making peace with John of Antioch, once he had satisfied himself that in spite of divergent modes of expression, their faith was identical."[81]

Somewhat similarly, on the occasion of the 1600th anniversary of the death of Saint Athanasius (1973), Pope Paul VI said in an address to Patriarch Shenouda: "He (Athanasius) in turn recognized in the Church of the West a secure identity of faith despite differences in vocabulary and in the theological approach to a deeper understanding of the mystery of the Triune God."[82]

---

[80] Vatican II, Decree on Ecumenism, No. 4; cf. Dogmatic Constitution on the Church, No. 23.

[81] Information Service, Secretariat for Promoting Christian Unity, 1967/3, p. 10. Similarly it is reported in the message of the Holy Father to the Ecumenical Patriarch that "it is a matter of knowing and of respecting each other in the legitimate diversity of liturgical, spiritual disciplinary and theological traditions (cf. council's Decree on Ecumenism, Nos. 14 and 17) by means of a frank theological dialogue, made possible by the re-establishment of brotherly charity in order to attain accord in the sincere confession of all revealed truths. In order to restore and preserve communion and unity, care must indeed be taken to 'impose no burden beyond what is indispensable' (Acts 15:28; council's Decree on Ecumenism, No. 18)."

[82] Information Service, Secretariat for Promoting Christian Unity, No. 22, October 1973/IV, p. 7.

63. Diversities — be they diversities of church traditions or diversities caused by specific historic, ethnic and cultural contexts — can be understood and lived as different forms of expressing the one and the same faith when they are "related to the central message of salvation and Christian faith" and do not endanger this centre,[83] and when they are therefore sustained by one and the same gospel. It is not necessary that each church adopt the specific forms of belief, piety or ethics of the other church and make them its own. But each church must recognize them as specific and legitimate forms of the one, common Christian faith. Then it is "justified to recognize a legitimate diversity in the plurality of traditions and to assess them positively".[84]

64. In this sense, for example, the Catholic-Lutheran dialogue on the eucharist has led to the result that the existing differences in the statements about the manner in which Christ is present in the eucharist "must no longer be regarded as opposed in a way that leads to separation", but that in common, albeit in different ways, "the reality of the eucharistic presence" is testified to.[85] Similarly, the Catholic-Lutheran dialogue document on the ministry in the church, with a view to the different interpretations and statements regarding "sacramentality" and "uniqueness" of ordination, was of the opinion that it could speak of a "consensus on the reality" as follows: "Wherever it is taught that through the act of ordination the Holy Spirit gives grace strengthening the ordained person for the life-time ministry of word and sacrament, it must be asked whether differences which previously divided the churches on this question have not been overcome."[86]

65. In the area of ethical decisions it appears important that the Catholic Church right up to and including the Council of Trent[87] did not condemn the practice of divorced persons remarrying in the Eastern Orthodox churches although it did reject this practice for itself.

66. The joint Catholic-Lutheran reflection on the Augsburg Confession must be seen in this context, as it proceeded during recent years and when

---

[83] Statement on "Models of Unity", *In Christ — A New Community*, op. cit., p. 174.

[84] Gemeinsame Synode der Bistümer der BRD, 1974, No. 4.33. The Assembly of the Lutheran World Federation (1977) spoke in this connection of "a way of living encounter, spiritual experience together, theological dialogue and mutual correction, a way on which the distinctiveness of each partner is not lost sight of but rings out, is transformed and renewed, and in this way becomes visible and palpable to the other partners as a legitimate form of Christian existence and of the one Christian faith". *In Christ — A New Community*, p. 174. Cf. No. 33 above.

[85] *The Eucharist*, No. 51; cf. Nos. 48–51 and 16.

[86] *The Ministry in the Church*, No. 33; cf. Nos. 32 and 39.

[87] Cf. Tridentinum, Sess. XXIV, canon 7; DS 1807 and Note 1.

it had become clear that as far as this confession is concerned — including its diverse expressions and approaches — one could note "full accord on fundamental and central truths".[88] Likewise, quite a few dogmatic decisions of the Catholic Church need a common and, if possible, binding interpretation that would bring out more clearly the common ground of our faith. This would be particularly true for the more recent dogmas relating to Mary and to the papacy, because for Lutheran churches and Christians to accept that they are in accordance with Scripture and gospel represents a serious problem.[89]

3. Removal of Doctrinal Condemnations

67. Our ecclesial awareness has been traumatized by mutual condemnations. These may have been uttered as formal, reciprocal doctrinal condemnations, but they can also be seen as general prejudices that have taken root in the consciousness of the members of our churches. It is precisely in this form that they have had particularly widespread and fateful repercussions. In order to return to a common confession of the one faith and a true communal relationship, it is necessary that each of our churches declare officially in all points where this is possible in view of the current teaching of the other church that these condemnations have become meaningless.

68. Past doctrinal condemnations cannot be rendered ineffectual through a relativizing of truth. Rather, it is the duty to be truthful which calls us to act.

Theological-historical research and more recent ecclesial developments lead us even now to the insight that in important questions those reciprocal doctrinal condemnations are not or are no longer applicable. Thus, for example, the necessary rejection by the Reformation of the "Pelagians and others who teach that, without the Holy Spirit and by the power of nature alone, we are able to love God above all things and can also keep the commandments of God in so far as the substance of the acts is concerned",[90] does not affect the official teaching of the Catholic

---

[88] Cf. No. 51 above; cf. "All Under One Christ", particularly Nos. 14f.

[89] With a view to Eastern Orthodox churches Joseph Cardinal Ratzinger says regarding the doctrine of primacy: "Rome does not have to require of the East more regarding the primacy doctrine than was formulated and practised during the first thousand years." Basically it can be said "that what was possible for a thousand years, cannot be impossible for Christians today" ("Die Frage der Wiedervereinigung zwischen Ost und West", *Theologische Prinzipienlehre,* op. cit., 209).

[90] CA XVIII, Ed. 1531, Book of Concord, p. 40.

Church.[91] Vice versa, the equally necessary Catholic rejection of those who hold that "Christians are not concerned with the Ten Commandments"[92] or that "anyone who has become justified once can no longer sin or lose his state of grace"[93] is not applicable to the position of the Lutheran confessions.[94] Similarly, the Reformation condemnation of "those who teach that the sacraments justify by the outward acts" and "without the proper attitude in the recipient"[95] is not applicable to Catholic teaching[96] and vice versa the Catholic rejection of those who say "that the sacraments of the New Covenant do not communicate grace *ex opere operato,* but that the faith alone is sufficient to obtain the grace of divine promise"[97] does not apply to the Lutheran confessions.[98] Moreover, the Reformation's condemnation of the sacrifice of the Mass as a denial of the once-for-all sacrifice of the cross[99] does not touch the teaching of the Catholic Church[100] any more than Catholic condemnation of those who deny the real presence of Christ in the eucharist[101] or call it into question by rejecting the doctrine of transubstantiation[102] need apply to the Lutheran church and its teaching.[103]

69. To be sure, agreement that earlier doctrinal condemnations are no longer applicable cannot be achieved by mere statements of consensus issued by theologians. What is really needed are official declarations by the chief teaching authorities of each of the churches concerned, each according to its own procedures. In the Catholic Church this falls within the competence of the Holy See in agreement with the episcopate as a whole. In the Lutheran churches the most appropriate procedure would be one analogous to what was done in accepting the Leuenberg Agreement, i.e., a form of synodal process in the individual churches (see Nos. 23–26 above).

---

[91] Cf. DS 1551–1553.

[92] DS 1569.

[93] DS 1573.

[94] Cf. CA XX, 1f., The Book of Concord, p. 41; CA XII, 7, The Book of Concord, p. 35; The Smalcald Articles, Part III, III, 42–45, The Book of Concord, pp. 309f.

[95] CA XIII, Ed. 1531, The Book of Concord, p. 36; Apology of the Augsburg Confession, IV, 63, The Book of Concord, p. 115.

[96] Cf. *The Eucharist,* No. 61; pp. 69–75.

[97] DS 1608.

[98] Cf. CA V, 2; VIII, 2; XIII; The Book of Concord, pp. 31, 33, 35f.; *The Eucharist,* pp. 70–73.

[99] The Smalcald Articles, Part II, II, The Book of Concord, pp. 293ff.

[100] Cf. *The Eucharist,* Nos. 56–61.

[101] DS 1651.

[102] Cf. DS 1652.

[103] Cf. *The Eucharist,* Nos. 14–17, 50–51.

Official declarations of this type, however, will gain their true ecclesial importance and find their way into the life of the people of God only if they happen in the framework of liturgical celebrations that give expression to both penitence and thanksgiving.

b. COMMUNITY IN SACRAMENTS

70. Community with Christ and community of Christians with each other are mediated through word and sacrament in the Holy Spirit. Where Christians and churches desire full community with each other, it follows that their joint understanding of the apostolic witness and their common testimony to the Christian faith (see 55ff. above) must go hand in hand with a common sacramental life.[104] We can note gratefully that in this respect important things have happened recently. (1) Our churches have a more intensive sacramental life. (2) With regard to understanding and celebration of the sacraments a growing agreement can be noted. The requirements for a common sacramental life have, however, not yet been fully met. (3) Within the fundamental consensus, open questions remain.

1. Growth of Sacramental Life in our Churches

71. In both the consciousness of Lutheran and Roman Catholic churches the sacramental dimension of the Christian life has in recent times once again come to the fore. Growing out of the sacrament of baptism (Rom 6:3ff.), Christian life in its deepest sense is the gift of sharing in the death and resurrection of Jesus Christ. This sharing is mediated through proclamation of the word and celebration of the sacraments equally.[105] In the sacraments it occurs in a manner which accents the corporeality, the personal character and the community dimension of this sharing, whereby it should be noted that for Lutherans as well as for Catholics the word belongs to the nature of the sacraments themselves.[106]

---

[104] Cf. *Ways to Community,* Nos. 14ff.

[105] Cf. Apology of the Augsburg Confession, XIII, 5, The Book of Concord, pp. 211f.; Vatican II, Dogmatic Constitution on Divine Revelation, No. 2; Decree on the Ministry and Life of Priests, Nos. 2 and 4; Constitution on the Sacred Liturgy, No. 7.

[106] Cf. Vatican II, Constitution on the Sacred Liturgy, No. 35; on the Lutheran side the reception of the sentence of St. Augustine: "*Accedat verbum ad elementum et fit sacramentum*" ("when the Word is added to the element or the natural substance, it becomes a sacrament"), for example in the Large Catechism IV, 18, The Book of Concord, p. 438, and in the Smalcald Articles, Part III, V, 1, The Book of Concord, p. 310.

72. The deepened consciousness of the sacramental dimension of Christian existence has also reshaped the life and practice of our churches.

In several respects the last few centuries have seen a renewal of sacramental life in the Roman Catholic Church.

— New emphasis has been placed on the interrelatedness of sacrament, proclaimed word and faith that the Reformers felt necessary to stress again.[107] This has influenced the reform of the liturgical orders for the celebration of the sacraments.

— The primary importance of baptism[108] and of the eucharist[109] has been stressed, especially by reshaping their celebration.

— A comprehensive view of the sacramental life of the church has been given precedence over an isolated approach to individual sacraments by understanding the church in Christ as "the universal sacrament of salvation"[110], as "the 'Sacrament of unity' ".[111]

These tendencies have led to liturgical developments which parallel many Lutheran concerns: greater space for the proclamation of the word of God, use of the vernacular, more frequent communion under both kinds, curtailing of masses without the participation of the people, to mention only the most important reforms.

73. Paralleling this, an intensification of sacramental life in the Lutheran churches has developed.

— Regarding baptism which in the Lutheran tradition has always been considered fully a sacrament and a fundamental and permanent point of reference of Christian existence, there is renewed appreciation of its place in the Sunday gathering for worship.

— The eucharist is today being celebrated more frequently at the regular Sunday worship service than was the case in the past. The Reformation had stressed that Lutheran communities celebrated it with par-

---

[107] Vatican II, Constitution on the Sacred Liturgy, Nos. 24, 35, 51, 52; *The Eucharist,* Nos 7 and 61.
[108] Vatican II, Dogmatic Constitution on the Church, No. 15; Decree on Ecumenism, No. 22.
[109] Ibid., Decree on the Church's Missionary Activity, No. 9; Decree on the Ministry and Life of Priests, No. 5.
[110] Ibid., Dogmatic Constitution on the Church, No. 48; cf. Nos. 1 and 9.
[111] Ibid., Constitution on the Sacred Liturgy, No. 26. In this respect present-day theology can speak of the church as the "primordial sacrament" and of Christ as the "proto-sacrament" in whom and through whom the church is the universal sacrament of salvation (Dogmatic Constitution on the Church, Nos. 1 and 48).

ticular devotion and reverence, expressly urging believers to communicate.[112]

— It is stressed that as far as the Lutheran tradition is concerned the sacramental dimension of Christian life was never called into question and, indeed, was expressly defended in inter-Reformation disputes. It was thus possible for the Lutheran Reformers — following the Scriptures (Col 1:27; 1 Tim 3:16) — to speak of Christ as the one sacrament[113] or to attribute "sacramental" character to the word of the Scripture and the proclaimed word as bearers of the presence of Christ and as efficacious word.[114]

74. The linkages of the sacraments and their liturgical celebrations both with the world and with all humanity have again been discovered by Lutheran and Catholic traditions together.[115]

2. Increasing Agreement in Understanding and Celebration of the Sacraments

75. Lutherans and Catholics are conscious that they participate in one and the same *baptism*.[116] In keeping with the statement BEM, we jointly confess that "Christian baptism is rooted in the ministry of Jesus of Nazareth, in his death and in his resurrection. It is incorporation into Christ, who is the crucified and risen Lord; it is entry into the New Covenant between God and God's people."[117] This common understanding of baptism is expressed in the manner in which baptism is administered and is confirmed by the fact that almost everywhere our churches have officially recognized each other's baptism. Moreover, our churches are faced by common or similar pastoral tasks concerning the understanding of baptism, and how it is expressed and concretized in baptismal practice, faith-life and the piety of congregations and the faithful.

76. A great deal of progress towards a common understanding and celebration of the *eucharist* has been made in recent years as a result of numerous dialogues between our churches at various levels. In the course

---

[112] CA XXIV, 1 and 4, The Book of Concord, p. 56.
[113] WA 6, 86; WA 6, 501, Luther's Works, American Edition, Philadelphia, 1959, vol. 36, p. 18; cf. Melanchthon's Loci communes theologici, *The Library of Christian Classics,* Melanchthon and Bucer, London, 1969, vol. XIX, p. 135.
[114] WA 9, 440–442.
[115] Cf. for example *The Eucharist,* Nos. 38–41.
[116] Cf. Vatican II, Dogmatic Constitution on the Church, No. 15; Decree on Ecumenism, Nos. 3, 4 and 22.
[117] *Baptism, Eucharist and Ministry,* Faith and Order Paper No. 111, Geneva 1982, Baptism, I, 1.

of these dialogues it proved possible to reconcile positions with regard to the understanding of the eucharist that had previously been thought to be in conflict and were therefore seen as divisive (sacrifice of the Mass, eucharistic presence); many of the remaining differences are within the common sphere, thus depriving them of their divisive force.[118] Regarding liturgical form, both churches are moving towards growing consensus in the basic elements of eucharistic celebration.[119]

77. Theological endeavours have also led to a better reciprocal understanding regarding the other sacraments in the Catholic Church, whose sacramental character has hitherto been admitted only hesitantly or not at all by the Lutheran churches.

78. Various Catholic-Lutheran dialogues on the ordained ministry in the church have shown that, even though Lutherans do not speak of *ordination* as a sacrament, there is yet "substantial convergence" between the Catholic and Lutheran understanding and practice wherever ordination is celebrated through the laying on of hands and prayer (*epiklesis*) as act of blessing and wherever it is taught "that through the act of ordination the Holy Spirit gives grace strengthening the ordained person for the life-time ministry of word and sacrament".[120] Lutheran tradition has taken account of this even though it does not include ordination among the sacraments in the strict sense. "In principle ... (it does) not reject" the sacramental understanding of ordination.[121]

79. The Augsburg Confession and both of Luther's catechisms treat *confession* (of sin) in close connection with the baptismal and eucharistic sacraments. In the Apology of the Augsburg Confession they are even expressly included among the sacraments.[122] Present-day Catholic-Lutheran research with regard to the understanding of confession in the Augsburg Confession, moreover, has brought to light misunderstandings of each other's position that existed on both sides in the sixteenth

---

[118] Cf. *The Eucharist,* and the document of the Catholic-Lutheran dialogue in the USA: The Eucharist: A Lutheran-Roman Catholic Statement, *Lutherans and Catholics in Dialogue,* III, "The Eucharist as Sacrifice", Washington/New York, 1967.
[119] Cf. *The Eucharist,* Nos. 75 and 76; "The Liturgical Celebration of the Eucharist", ibid., pp. 29ff.
[120] *The Ministry in the Church,* No. 33; cf. No. 32; also Malta-Report, No. 59; and the document of the Catholic-Lutheran dialogue in the USA: Eucharist and Ministry: A Lutheran-Roman Catholic Statement, *Lutherans and Catholics in Dialogue,* IV, Washington/New York, 1970, No. 16.
[121] *The Ministry in the Church,* No. 33.
[122] Apology of the Augsburg Confession XIII, 4, The Book of Concord, p. 211.

century.[123] The Roman Catholic liturgy of penitence, which places the accent on the remission of sins and on personal guidance together with the more frequent celebration of penitence, foreseen in the new Catholic liturgy, help to promote understanding between our two churches. The difficulties encountered today by the practice of personal confession in certain areas of the Catholic Church, and the widespread lack of understanding among many Lutherans make confession a common pastoral task for both churches.

80. Our dialogue about marriage and mixed marriages has revealed a "view of marriage which is in a profound sense a common one". We affirm together that the event of salvation in Christ affects Christians also in their conjugal life which can never be without reference to it. The relationship is nothing other than the grace "as a lasting promise", which Christ grants people in their married life, a grace that "is not simply an idea" but "reality". This means, however, attributing to marriage a "sacramental" aspect, a "sacramental power", even though the Reformation churches do not consider it "to be a sacrament in the full sense of the word".[124]

81. Confirmation and the anointing of the sick have received hardly any consideration in the Catholic-Lutheran dialogue.

Since in the Western churches *confirmation* developed into a rite distinct from baptism, the questions regarding the necessary age for its administration and its precise function have been discussed again and again. In the Lutheran Reformation confirmation disappeared completely. Later it was reintroduced as a rite of admission to the Lord's Supper and/or the celebration of coming of age. As such it was closely linked with previous catechetical instruction. In the Catholic Church confirmation is understood to be an integral part of sacramental initiation into the church, although here, too, it is not devoid of catechetical aspects. In both churches the promise of the gifts of the Holy Spirit is central. Even in the Lutheran understanding confirmation is an act of blessing performed through the prayer of the congregation, and in which grace is promised and granted to the confirmand. Catholics and Lutherans both participate in the ecumenical discussion of the questions about a proper relationship of confirmation to baptism and Christian witness.[125]

---

[123] H. Fagerberg/H. Jorissen, "Busse und Beichte", *Confessio Augustana – Bekenntnis des einen Glaubens,* edited by H. Meyer/H. Schütte, Paderborn/Frankfurt, 1980, pp. 228ff.
[124] *Theology of Marriage and the Problems of Mixed Marriages,* Geneva, 1977, Nos. 16–21 and 29.
[125] *Baptism, Eucharist and Ministry,* op. cit., Baptism, No. 14.

82. In the course of postconciliar reforms in the Catholic Church the *anointing of the sick* was emphasized more strongly than before as a special help for the sick and the dying, and it was linked with the proclamation of the word. Lutherans have seldom practised the anointing of the sick. They have, however, attributed great importance to the pastoral care of sick people. In some Lutheran churches this has recently led to attempts to reintroduce anointing of the sick.[126] This could therefore become the subject of a promising dialogue between Catholics and Lutherans if one bears in mind the common pastoral tasks and the emerging rapprochement. Both, Catholics and Lutherans, are now finding a point of encounter inasmuch as the former are gradually getting away from an isolated understanding of the individual sacraments, and the latter are more and more abandoning a narrow use of the concept of sacrament. This, in order to understand and live together the sacramental dimension of Christian existence in a new and better way. Particularly in the present situation where people experience social isolation and personal loneliness, both traditions have a special pastoral task towards the sick and the dying.

3. Open Questions, Remaining Differences, Basic Agreements

83. In spite of an enhanced common awareness of the sacramental dimension of Christian and ecclesial life and in spite of a deepened consensus in the understanding and praxis of the sacraments, there remain open questions that must be answered with a view to the common sacramental life that belongs to full church fellowship. Clarification of these questions must be brought about in joint dialogue and in the life and praxis of each of the two churches. In this connection the agreements which already exist or which we have now reached, give us the freedom to challenge each other and to ask reciprocally critical questions regarding teaching and praxis.

84. Nevertheless, even here we must not strive after a questionable homogeneity. Just as in the case of the understanding of faith, the common sacramental life needed for unity must not be mistaken for uniformity. Room must be left for legitimate diversities. This is true not only in relation to the understanding and shaping of the individual sacraments or sacramental ecclesial acts, but also in relation to the concept of sacrament as such. The open questions remaining, especially regarding the number of sacraments, are ultimately rooted in an open concept of sacrament. Not only between our two churches, but also

---

[126] *Occasional Services,* A Companion to Lutheran Book of Worship, Minneapolis and Philadelphia, 1982, "Service of the Word for Healing", pp. 89–102.

within our churches the concept of sacrament is not fixed in every last detail. A certain fluctuation historically in determining the number of sacraments as well as the differentiation between or "ranking" of the sacraments[127] (and a conjunctive "analogue-use" of the sacramental concept) — all point in this direction.

85. For an understanding and the celebration of the individual sacraments and therefore also for the common sacramental life of our two churches, it has to be taken into account that the sacraments are part of God's trinitarian act of salvation: the work that God performed in Christ once for all for the salvation of the world is mediated by the Holy Spirit who works through word and sacrament so that *communio sanctorum* is formed, i.e., church as participation in the gifts of salvation and as communion of the faithful.

This makes it clear once more how important it is for a proper understanding and conservation of the sacramental dimension of Christian existence and church life when both our traditions are able to speak of Christ as the one sacrament and therefore as the source of the individual sacraments (see Nos. 72 and 73 above). At the same time it becomes clear why on the Catholic side one speaks today of the church as the "sacrament".[128] The Lutheran tradition is not yet very familiar with this thought, and it is often inclined to criticize it. But its intention should be acceptable for Lutherans: as the body of Christ and "koinonia" of the Holy Spirit, the church is the sign and instrument of God's grace, an instrument that of itself can do nothing. The church lives by the word as it lives by the sacraments and at the same time stands in their service.

c. COMMUNITY OF SERVICE

86. The church lives by word and sacrament and also stands in their service. It has therefore a structured form in which the service of the whole people of God and the service of those who have been entrusted with the special ordained ministry can act together. Consequently, in our search for church fellowship, it is not possible to separate the efforts for community of faith (II/a) and sacramental life (II/b) from efforts for a

---

[127] Baptism and eucharist as "chief basic sacraments", *Ways to Community,* No. 18; cf. Tridentinum, DS 1603; Vatican II, Dogmatic Constitution on the Church, No. 7, and the concept of *potissima sacramenta* of Thomas Acquinas (S.Th. III q. 62, a.5) or the *sacramenta maiora.*
[128] Cf. Vatican II, Dogmatic Constitution on the Church, Nos. 1, 9, 48; Constitution on the Sacred Liturgy, No. 26.

structured church fellowship (community of service) that would permit and ensure common life, common decisions and common action (see No. 49 above).

1. Commitment to a Structured Fellowship (Community of Service)

87. If in the present process of growing reciprocal recognition and reception our two churches affirm increasingly that they confess the same faith and share a common understanding of the sacraments, then they are also entitled and obliged to enter into structured fellowship with each other. With the New Testament we confess the church as "people of God", as "body of Christ" and as "temple of the Holy Spirit". This confession does not permit us to limit the relationship between our churches to be a mere reciprocally respectful coexistence or internalization. This confession calls us to live out the existing community of faith and sacrament also in a structured ecclesial fellowship. Each of these images of the church, found in the New Testament, confronts us with this commitment.

88. The church as *people of God* is called to live in unity, for God does not lead Christians to himself and to salvation in isolation or independently of each other. Faith, without ceasing to be personal faith, is always a faith that lives in the community and is transmitted, preserved and renewed in it. Just as the people of the Old Covenant encompassed different tribes and yet was one single people of God, the new people of God has been called together from all nations of the earth, embraces all the diversity of the human world, lives in many places, and listens to God's calling in many languages and in many different ways. It is nevertheless a single undivided people, called by the one Lord, in the one Spirit, to one faith, to solidarity and love for each other, and to common witness and service in the world.

89. The church, the new "people of God", is the *body of Christ*. "For by one Spirit we were all baptized into one body" (1 Cor 12:13). Elsewhere, speaking of the eucharist, Saint Paul says: "The bread which we break, is it not a participation in the body of Christ? Because there is one bread, we who are many are one body" (1 Cor 10:16f.). Just as the eucharist is not a part of the body of Christ but the whole Christ, so also the local church is not only a part of the whole, but a realization of the church of God.[129] If therefore according to the New Testament the in-

---

[129] This theological principle describes the relationship among the local churches in New Testament times and also the relationship of the local churches within the Catholic Church according to the understanding of Vatican II: "This Church of ▶

dividual local church is church of God in the *full* sense, it is yet not the *whole* church of God. This limited nature of the individual churches and their necessary solidarity with each other calls for a concrete and lived-out fellowship which embraces all aspects of ecclesial life. It corresponds to the nature of the church which as "body of Christ" is an organic whole.

90. Just as the church is called to be "people of God" and "body of Christ", it is also called to be *temple of the Holy Spirit*. Since the plenitude of the gifts of the Spirit is given only in the fellowship of all local churches, no church can claim the Holy Spirit for itself alone.[130] Such a claim would contradict the fellowship instituted by the Holy Spirit. The same would be true if one single church wanted to live a life independent of the other churches, if it wanted to dominate them, or even if it were indifferent towards the faith of these churches. Confessing the church as "temple of the Holy Spirit" and recognizing the other church as "temple of the Holy Spirit" means therefore entering into active fellowship with

---

Christ is truly present in all legitimate local congregations of the faithful, which, united with their pastors, are themselves called churches" (Dogmatic Constitution on the Church, No. 26). "In and from such individual churches there comes into being the one and only Catholic Church" (ibid., No. 23; cf. Decree on the Bishops' Pastoral Office in the Church, No. 11). The application of this principle to the Catholic Church and the Lutheran churches must be regarded as legitimate from the moment — but only from the moment — they have found their way back to community in faith and sacramental life universally or locally.

[130] Vatican II, Dogmatic Constitution on the Church, No. 13 interprets the words (1 Pet 4:10): "As each has received a gift, employ it for one another as good stewards of God's varied grace" pneumatologically and applies them to the local churches. In the spirit of this theological principle, the Dogmatic Constitution on the Church, No. 13, adds that in the people of God "each individual part of the Church contributes through its special gifts to the good of the other parts and of the whole Church. Thus through the common sharing of gifts and through the common effort to attain fullness in unity, the whole and each of the parts receive increase."

Such a theological principle can be applied to the relationship between the Catholic Church and the Lutheran churches. Re-established unity in faith and in the sacraments enables them jointly to share in the dynamic which the Dogmatic Constitution on the Church, No. 13, describes as follows: "Moreover, within the Church particular Churches hold a rightful place. These Churches retain their own traditions without in any way lessening the primacy of the Chair of Peter. This Chair presides over the whole assembly of charity and protects legitimate differences, while at the same time it sees that such differences do not hinder unity but rather contribute toward it. Finally, between all the parts of the Church there remains a bond of close communion with respect to spiritual riches, apostolic workers, and temporal resources."

this church. If one and the same spirit of love and unity lives in the churches, all are obliged to pray for each other, to work together and to care for each other.

91. The growing reciprocal recognition as church thus leads us to binding common life, to active exchange and to mutual acceptance in witness, service and solidarity according to the nature of the church as "people of God", "body of Christ" and "temple of the Holy Spirit". It commits our churches at both the local and the universal levels not only to an occasional fellowship, practised from time to time, but to a fully lived-out fellowship that requires for its realization a structured form.

2. Structured Church Fellowship and a Common Ordained Ministry

92. The dialogue between our churches and, in general, ecumenical efforts for visible unity of the church have shown that the structured form needed for full and binding fellowship between churches can be manifold and variable. It is not limited to the hierarchical dimension of the church, but rather embraces the service of the whole people of God, includes the charisms of all the faithful, and expresses itself in synodal structures and processes. At the same time, fellowship in the ordained ministry forms an essential part of the structured church fellowship.

This fellowship in the ordained ministry, though not yet fully realized, is nevertheless basically present in the mutual recognition of ministries as forms of the ministry instituted by Christ.[131] The coexistence of ministries mutually recognized must be transformed into a common exercise of ordained ministry appropriate to its nature, whereby particular importance is attached to the common exercise of the "ministry of leadership and of pastoral supervision (*episcopé*)".[132]

Only in a church fellowship so structured, is it possible to take joint decisions to preserve and further the apostolicity, catholicity and unity of the church and to act jointly in witness and service.

93. There already exists today a broad area in which a partial common exercise of ordained ministry and also of ecclesial *episkopé* is possible, desirable and even necessary. It is carried out between our two churches, for example, in the area of social responsibility, in the ethical, diaconal and charitable fields, or in evangelization.

---

[131] Cf. *The Ministry in the Church*, No. 85.
[132] Ibid., Nos. 42, 43 and 44.

94. But yet these forms of cooperation between ordained ministries are far from a comprehensive, fully common exercise of the ordained ministry. In order to have progress, one must look at three factors:

(1) the statement of Vatican II which regarding the ordained ministry of the Reformation churches speaks of a "lack of the sacrament of orders";[133]

(2) a certain "asymmetry" in the more precise definition of the theological value assigned to the ministry, particularly of the historic episcopacy in the understanding of the church;

(3) the close bond that exists in the Catholic Church between the bishops and the Pope.

95.(1) While according to the Lutheran understanding of church, the existence of the ministry in the Catholic Church is not to be called into question,[134] Catholics cannot yet fully recognize the ordained ministry in Lutheran churches because, according to their view, these churches lack the fullness of the ordained ministry since they "lack of the sacrament of orders".[135] This would only be possible through a process of "acceptance of full church communion",[136] of which fellowship in the historical episcopacy is an essential part.

96.(2) Catholics and Lutherans share the conviction that the ordained ministry of the church which, because it is "instituted by Jesus Christ"[137] "stands over against the community as well as within the community",[138] is "essential" for the church.[139] Nevertheless it is *possible* for Lutherans, and in this they differ from Catholics, to give a theological description of the church without making explicit mention of the ministry, because it is either "presupposed"[140] or implied by the proclamation of the word and the administration of the sacraments.

97. Lutherans, like Catholics, can recognize as "the action of the Spirit"[141] the historical differentiation of the one apostolic ministry into more local ministry and more regional forms, and they can consider "the

---

[133] Vatican II, Decree on Ecumenism, No. 22.
[134] *The Ministry in the Church*, No. 79.
[135] Ibid., Nos. 75–78.
[136] Ibid., No. 82.
[137] Ibid., No. 20.
[138] Ibid., No. 23.
[139] Ibid., No. 17.
[140] Ibid., No. 30.
[141] Ibid., No. 45.

function of *episcopé* ... as necessary for the church".[142] Likewise, Lutherans feel free "to face up to the call for communion with the historic episcopal office",[143] i.e., the historically evolved pattern of episcopal ministry in the form of the office of bishop standing in apostolic succession. Nevertheless, Lutherans and Catholics place different accents on the significance of that historic episcopal office for the church.[144]

98. The two problems are closely related: The "lack of the sacrament of orders" that the Catholic side claims to be inherent in the ministry of the Lutheran churches cannot, because of its very nature, be annulled solely by theological insights and agreements or by ecclesiastical or canonical declarations and decisions, as, for example, by the theological and canonical act of recognizing these ministries. What is needed, rather, is acceptance of the fellowship in ecclesial ministry, and this, ultimately, means acceptance of the fellowship in episcopal ministry which stands in apostolic succession. Lutherans are fundamentally free and open to accept such fellowship in the episcopal office. Yet within this understanding of the importance or significance of the episcopal office for the catholicity, apostolicity and unity of the church, Lutherans are inclined to place the accent differently from Catholics.

99. The problems mentioned here need not block the road to fellowship in the church ministry and therefore to a fully structured ecclesial fellowship. But it does call for renewal and deepening of the understanding of the ordained ministry, particularly the ministry serving the unity and governance (*episcopé*) of the church.

100.(3) In connection with the above mentioned it has to be borne in mind that as far as Catholics are concerned fellowship in the ordained ministry is expressed by the college of all bishops with the Pope at its head.

101. A Roman Catholic bishop or a group of Catholic bishops do not exercise their *episcopé* without involving the whole of the episcopate.[145] When bishops intend to take a decision committing them and their church to a process which has as its goal full church fellowship with Lutheran churches, they can only do this in community with the whole of the Catholic episcopate. The same is true if within their own church they wish to concretize a common exercise of *episcopé* with their Lutheran partners.

---

[142] Ibid., No. 43.
[143] Ibid., No. 80.
[144] Cf. ibid., Nos. 43 and 66.
[145] Cyprian said: "The episcopate is one, each part of which is held by each one for the whole", "The Treatises of Cyprian", I, 5, *The Writings of the Ante-Nicene Fathers,* vol. 5, Grand Rapids, 1965, p. 423.

102. In concrete terms this means that the bishops exercise *episcopé* in the fellowship collegially with the first among them, the Pope. They recognize the supreme jurisdictional authority of the Pope over the universal church and all the faithful, an authority that — according to Vatican I — is of an episcopal, ordinary, and direct nature.[146]

103. The process that is to lead to a common ordained ministry via the joint exercise of the *episcopé* therefore necessarily requires the participation of the Pope. He can, in the face of the entire Roman Catholic Church, guarantee the propriety of this process. He can help assure that the unity re-established in one place will not lead to new divisions in another. Thus, according to its mission, the Petrine ministry can not only protect fellowship but further it.

---

[146] With respect to Catholic ecclesiology these terms have to be understood as follows:
— They do not mean that the Pope became the bishop of the Catholic Church as a result of the First Vatican Council. The signature of Paul VI under the documents of Vatican II identifies him as the bishop of the Catholic Church in Rome (cf. H. Marot, "Note sur l'expression 'episcolus ecclesiae catholicae' ", *Irénikon,* 37, 1964, pp. 221–226; again mentioned in Y. Congar (editor), "La collégialité épiscopale. Histoire et théologie", *Unam Sanctam,* 37, Paris, 1965, pp. 94–98.
— Nor do they mean that the Pope can take the place of the local bishops daily and permanently because, like the primacy, the episcopate exists by "the same divine institution" (cf. the collective declaration of the German episcopate regarding the circular letter of the German Chancellor concerning the future election of the Pope, DS 3112–3116, and the letter of approval by Pius IX).
— Finally they do not mean that there is no distinction between his commission as Primate of the Catholic Church and his task as Patriarch of the West. Thus, for example, the code *Juris Canonici* promulgated in 1983 is valid only for the Latin church. The bilateral dialogue between the Catholic Church and the Orthodox churches will probably induce the Holy See to determine which of its present functions belong to the primacy and which to the Patriarchate of the West.
And yet these expressions confirm the fact that the Catholic bishops always exercise their ministries in fellowship with the Bishop of Rome and that the Pope, in turn, exercises his ministry of unity and leadership within the college of bishops and the community of the churches thanks to the universal jurisdictional authority that is associated with his commission. This authority is defined as "ordinary" not in the sense of "daily" but in the sense of "not delegated", because it is part of his commission. The point of the primacy is not the day-to-day government of the church but to serve its unity.

3. Joint Reflection on the Early Church

104. The understanding of a ministry serving the unity of the church and *episcopé,* on which Catholics and Lutherans diverge to some extent, can be deepened and gain in commonality, if the two sides reflect together about how this ministry was seen and practised in the Early Church. Both sides have good reasons for participating in such a reflection.

105. According to the statements of Vatican II on the sacramentality and collegiality of the episcopal office,[147] Catholics no longer follow the view that prevailed in the Middle Ages. Taking the presbyterate (*sacerdotium*) as point of departure, it differentiated the episcopate only by virtue of its greater dignity and jurisdictional authority. One indication of this is the fact that in the 1968 edition of the *Pontificale Romanum* the former prayer accompanying the imposition of hands is replaced by the prayer taken from Hippolytus' *Apostolic Tradition.* Within Catholic theology this return to the early church fathers is also a call to emphasize more strongly the collegiality of the bishops as an expression of the fellowship of local churches.

106. The Lutheran Reformation basically affirmed the episcopal office of the Early Church.[148] There was readiness to retain the episcopal office in its traditional form, even though there was criticism of the manner in which the office was exercised at that time. To some extent this criticism was explicitly associated with and legitimated by references to the Early Church.[149] Thus it is clear that also on the Lutheran side the question of episcopal ministry is dealt with in reference to the Early Church.

107. The understanding of the nature of episcopal ministry which then prevailed becomes obvious in the rite of ordination of a bishop (see excursus "Ordination Practice in the Early Church"). Essential aspects of this are also significant for us today:

108. a. Ordination is at the same time a charismatic, liturgical and ecclesial event.

The Early Church did not separate the charismatic event (gift of the Spirit) from the liturgical ceremony (imposition of hands as part of the

---

[147] Vatican II, Dogmatic Constitution on the Church, Nos. 21f.
[148] Apology of the Augsburg Confession XIV, 1, The Book of Concord, p. 214; The Smalcald Articles, Part III, X, The Book of Concord, p. 314; The Formula of Concord, Solid Declaration, X, 19, The Book of Concord, p. 614; cf. *The Ministry in the Church,* No. 42.
[149] CA XXVIII, 28, The Book of Concord, p. 85; The Smalcald Articles, Part II, IV, The Book of Concord, pp. 298ff.; Treatise on the Power and Primacy of the Pope, 13–15, 62f., 70f., The Book of Concord, pp. 322, 330f., 331f.

eucharistic service on Sundays) nor from its ecclesial context (commissioning and jurisdiction). In the worshipping community and by the imposition of hands of the bishops, the new bishop receives the gift of the Spirit.[150] This gift contains a special charism of presiding over his church.[151]

109. The bishop is a baptized member of the local koinonia.[152] In the ordination he, as one who is baptized, receives the call of the church and induction into an office. These two aspects are linked by the action of the Holy Spirit, through which the new bishop receives a gift of grace, which is not intended for his own well-being and does not separate him from the congregation, but which is rather for the benefit of the congregation and which places him in its service.[153]

At the local level bishops stand in their churches and serve them as a *personal* responsibility. The particular responsibility of one bishop is thus linked with the responsibility of all, as is also shown by the ordination liturgy.

110. b. The vigilance with regard to the apostolicity of the faith that belongs to the bishop's duty, is bound up with the responsibility for the faith borne by the whole Christian people.

Members of the church participate in the election of their bishop and receive the person who is to exercise the apostolic ministry. In addition, when the candidate answers the ordination questions and confesses his faith in the presence of the congregation, the congregation is witness that the bishop represents the authentic apostolic faith. All this shows that the apostolic succession is not really to be understood as a succession of one individual to another,[154] but rather as a succession in the church, to

---

[150] That all may be "praying in their heart for the descent of the Spirit", *The Apostolic Tradition of Hippolytus*. Archon Books, Ann Arbor, Michigan, 1962, No. 2, p. 33.

[151] "Pneuma hegemonikon", ibid., No. 3, pp. 34f.

[152] Cf. Augustine: "Pro vobis episcopus, vobiscum christianus" (PL 38, 1483).

[153] Cf. the continuation of the quotation of Augustine: "Illud est nomen suscepti officii, illud gratiae" (PL 38, 1483).

[154] The canons do not permit a bishop to ordain his successor (cf. canon 75 of the so-called Apostolic Canons, Bruns I, 11; Synod of Antioch, 341, canon 23, Bruns I, 86; Synod of Caesarea, 393, see E.W. Brooks, The Sixth Book of the Letters of Severus Patriarch of Antioch, London Oxford, 1903, vol. II, pp. 223–224; Roman Synod, 465, canon 5, Bruns II, pp. 283–284). See also the statement made by Augustine who found himself in an embarrassing situation, since his bishop Valerian had asked him to be not "his successor, but ... be associated with him as coadjutor", and he had been ordained by Megalius, Primate of Numidia. Augustine excuses Valerian on the grounds that canon 8 of Nicea which does not allow the coexistence of two Catholic bishops in the same ▶

an episcopal see and to membership of the episcopal college,[155] as shown by the lists of bishops.[156]

The responsibility of the congregation is not limited to the moment of ordination. Its full scope is illustrated by the exception that "one must deny one's consent even to bishops when it happens that they err and speak in a manner that contradicts the canonical texts".[157] This means that the *episcopé* is not exercised in isolation but normally in concert with the community of the believers, i.e., within a diversity of ministries and services and in the *synodal* life of the local church.

111. c. The bishops are servants of unity and of the fellowship among churches.

Even though the Christians in a given place must give their consent in the election of their bishop, they do not impose their hands at his ordination. That is done by the leaders of the neighbouring churches.

Bishops thus both represent the universal church in their own church and represent their own church among all other churches.[158] This mediating position corresponds to the task of the new bishop in the realm of faith which is expressly emphasized by the confession-like structure of his ordination. As leader of his own church together with the other bishops (collegiality), he is to bear witness to the faith received from the apostles and to watch over it.

Furthermore, the bishops are those who primarily, though not exclusively, ensure regular communication between the churches. This is done

---

town, was not known in Hippo (*The Fathers of the Church, Early Christian Biographies*, Washington D.C., 1952, "The Life of St. Augustine by Bishop Possidius", chapt. 8, p. 82; PL 32, 39–40).

[155] Cf. *The Ministry in the Church*, No. 62.

[156] Episcopal lists are lists of those who preside over a church (cf. L. Koep, *Bischofslisten*, RAC 2, pp. 410–415). This connection between succession and tradition *within* a church has always been stressed jointly by Catholics and Orthodox (cf. the second session of the Joint International Commission for Theological Dialogue between the Roman Catholic Church and the Orthodox Church, Munich 1982: "The minister is also the one who 'receives' from his church, which is faithful to tradition, the word he transmits" (Information Service, op. cit., No. 49, 1982, II/III, p. 110).

[157] Augustin, *De unitate ecclesiae* 11, 28, PL 43, 410–411. Cf. also Thomas Aquinas, *De veritate quaestio*, q. 14 a, 10 ad 11: "And we believe the successors of the apostles and the prophets only in so far as they tell us those things which the apostles and prophets have left in their writings" (*Truth*, Chicago, 1952/4, vol. 2, p. 258).

[158] Vatican II says: "Each individual bishop represents his own church, but all of them together in union with the Pope represent the entire Church" (Dogmatic Constitution on the Church, No. 23).

formally in regional or even universal conciliar life that serves to further or re-establish fellowship among the churches.

Finally, bishops are obliged to promote the common action and common witness of the churches. All this indicates that the episcopal office, as understood in the light of ordination, must be exercised collegially if it is to serve the fellowship of the churches.

4. The Significance of Reflection on the Early Church for Church Fellowship Between Catholics and Lutherans

112. This understanding by the Early Church of the episcopal office as a service to the *koinonia* can stimulate, correct and enlarge the view of Catholics and Lutherans in their endeavours for a commonly exercised *episcopé*. It becomes particularly clear that *episcopé* is exercised in concert with the church as a whole in a personal, collegial and communal way. Consequently, the exercise of the *episcopé* cannot be separated from the responsibility of the laity or from "synodality" or conciliarity.

113. In the sense of the Early Church the episcopal office is to serve the *koinonia* of the local church in a threefold manner:

— *Personal:* Christ "came not to be served but to serve" (Mk 10:45). This is the duty of all Christians. It is particularly applicable to bishops in an office for which they have received grace, authority and responsibility. This personal dimension of *episcopé* excludes any purely administrative or functional interpretation of this ministry. Since it serves the diversity of gifts granted to Christians and the mission of the people of God, the incumbents themselves are not in the centre. Accordingly the linkage between the person of the incumbent and the commission of the office is properly balanced, and former misunderstandings can be eliminated.[159]

— *Collegial,* in the sense that one is never bishop for oneself, but in collegiality with the priests and deacons and in a college with the fellow-bishops. On the basis of ordination a bishop becomes bishop of the church over which he presides, and at the same time is recognized as bishop by the whole church and shares responsibility for it. When churches are in communion, ordination and full ecclesial recognition go hand in hand. From this follows the fully sanctioned

---

[159] Approaches in this direction can be found in P.E. Persson, *Kyrkans ämbete som Kristusrepresentation,* Lund, 1961 (shortened German version: Representatio Christi. *Der Amtsbegriff in der neueren römisch-katholischen Theologie,* Göttingen, 1966) and in L.M. Dewailly, "La personne du ministre et l'objet du ministère" (about Persson's book), *RSPhTh* 46, 1962, pp. 650–657.

participation of the bishops in the conciliar life of the church of God at both its regional and universal levels.

— *In cooperation with the congregation,* inasmuch as the bishop's ministry, even though it is not exercised in the name of the people, is generally exercised in fellowship with the people and respects the diversity of the ministries and charisms given by the Spirit.[160] Thus absolute sovereignty either on the part of the congregation or the bishop is excluded.

114. These three ways of exercising the bishop's ministry correspond to what the New Testament teaches us about the manner in which the apostles themselves exercised their ministry.[161]

---

[160] Note how Cyprian wanted to exercise his authority together with the Christians of his community, priests and deacons, and the college of bishops, i.e., in a synodal and collegial manner: "From the beginning of my episcopate, I decided to do nothing of my own opinion privately without your advice and the consent of the people" (Saint Cyprian, *Letters 1–81,* Washington D.C., 1964, Letter 14,4, p. 43). "I think that I alone ought not to give a decision in this matter ... since this examination of each one must be discussed and investigated more fully, not only with my colleagues, but with the whole people themselves" (ibid., Letter 34,4, p. 89; cf. Letter 19,2, pp. 52f.). Regarding the relationship between the bishop and his congregation in a number of large episcopal sees in the time of the Early Church, see L. Scipioni, Vescovo e popolo, Milano, Vita e Pensiero, 1977; regarding the Middle Ages, see Y. Congar, "Quod omnes tangit ab omnibus tractari ac approbari debet", *RHDFE* 4ᵉ série, 36, 1958, pp. 210–259, reprinted in *Droit ancien et structures ecclésiales, Variorum Reprints,* London, 1982.

[161] Their ministry can be exercised in a *personal* manner, which is shown very clearly in the letters of Saint Paul. Behind the statements and instructions of Paul lie the grace and function given to him personally (cf. the expression "by the grace given to me" in Rom 12:3 and 15:15; 1 Cor 3:10; Gal 2:9; [see also Col 1:25; Eph 3:2,7f.] and from the greetings Rom 1:1; 1 Cor 1:1; 2 Cor 1:1; Gal 1:1; [cf. also Col 1:1; Eph 1:1] regarding the topic, cf. Gal 1). Paul also needs the *koinonia* of the other apostles if his preaching is to be not in vain (cf. Gal 2:1–10, especially verse 9; 1 Cor 15:7f.).

This *collegiality* of the (twelve) apostles appears particularly in the Acts of the Apostles which speaks stereo-typically of "the apostles" (in plural — 26 times) and where they are often presented as a body acting homogeneously (cf. Acts 2:42f.; 4:33,35,36f.; 5:12; 6:6; 8:14,18; 11:1. Occasionally Peter appears as protagonist of the apostles: cf. Acts 2:14,37; 5:2f., 29). It is noteworthy that the exercise of authority by the apostles by no means excludes the cooperation of the *presbyters* and the *congregation,* but proceeds in "concerted action", as is expressly the case at the election of the "seven" (Acts 6:2–6) and is shown even more clearly in connection with the so-called Council of Apostles (cf. Acts 15:2,4,22f.; 16:4). Note also the justification of Peter before "the apostles and the brethren who were in Judea" (Acts 11:1–18). This *koinonia* with the congregation in the exercise of the ministry is less directly expressed but is substantially present in a more nuanced way in the letters of Paul. These letters give evidence of great respect for the ▶

They have also been underscored repeatedly in the wider ecumenical endeavours.[162]

Also within our churches corresponding new deliberations are taking place.

115. Since the Second Vatican Council the Catholic Church has been introducing institutional changes which stress the coresponsibility of parishioners in the local churches. Various councils have been set up to bring together the local pastors and members (parish councils), the bishop and the faithful in his diocese (pastoral councils) and the bishop and the presbyters (presbyteral councils). Likewise, diocesan and regional synods have been held with the participation of laity. The functions of the bishops are thus being combined in a structured manner with the responsibility of the whole people of God and its various members.

116. The realization of a true communal life which corresponds to the nature of the church as a fellowship (*koinonia*) is an important current concern of the Lutheran churches. Efforts are thus being made — partly by referring to the insights of the Reformation which stress again the Early Church's concept of the priesthood of all the baptized — to meet the dangers of a "clerical church" by trying to further the participation and active responsibility of all parish members. In the emphasis on the

---

responsibility of the congregation in spite of their stress on the authority of the apostle. Paul (usually) does not decree, but argues (indicative — imperative!) and thus takes the congregation at their word regarding their own Christian freedom. It is striking that apart from specific questions of faith, Paul hardly ever gives his *own* instructions regarding the concrete ordering of the practical life of the congregation, but only intervenes when the praxis of the congregation errs. That in this respect Paul understands his authority as subsidiary to the authority of the congregation is expressed clearly in 1 Cor 5 and 6:1–12, where he does not appeal to the "offenders", but to the congregation which should really have acted on its own.

[162] The BEM statement on the Ministry (1982) notes: "The ordained ministry should be exercised in a personal, collegial and communal way" (No. 26). This is developed by stressing the complementarity of these three aspects, and it is added: "An appreciation of these three dimensions lies behind a recommendation made by the first World Conference on Faith and Order at Lausanne in 1927: 'In view of (i) the place which the episcopate, the council of presbyters and the congregation of the faithful, respectively, had in the constitution of the early Church, and (ii) the fact that episcopal, presbyteral and congregational systems of government are each today, and have been for centuries, accepted by great communions of Christendom, and (iii) the fact that episcopal, presbyteral and congregational systems are each believed by many to be essential to the good order of the Church, we therefore recognize that these several elements must all, under conditions which require further study, have an appropriate place in the order of life of a reunited Church ...' " (Commentary, No. 26).

local congregation assembled by God through word and sacrament, which is characteristic of the Lutheran understanding of church, evidences of a congregational narrowness are today seen with a more critical eye than in former times, and efforts are being made to counteract them theologically and practically. The enhanced awareness of the importance of the *episcopé,* clearly to be seen among Lutherans, must be noted in this connection. It is understood however not as a mere administrative office, but as a ministry of word and sacrament, and particularly as ministry of the *pastor pastorum* which serves the wider ecclesial fellowship and becomes its effective representative.

5. Approach to a Jointly Exercised Ministry of Fellowship

117. Common reflection about the Early Church brings to light a way to a jointly exercised ministry which requires careful examination. The following considerations may be of help. The proposed process is not necessarily the only possible one, though it does seem to avoid obstacles which have, up to now, impeded the way to church fellowship. The description here given may be modified in many of its details. It is neither a rigid nor a final plan. Preserving its central intention however is what is important.

118. The process leading to full realization of church fellowship as a structured community is, strictly speaking, a correlated and integral process involving reciprocally recognized ministries and the joint exercise of ministries, especially of the ministry of the *episcopé.*[163] Fully spelt out, it has the following structure:

An officially declared mutual recognition of ordained ministries opens the way by means of an initial act to the joint exercise of *episcopé,* including ordaining. A series of such ordinations would eventually lead to a common ordained ministry. The process could function at the universal level, but could also be set in motion at local, regional or national ecclesial levels.

The process would thus have the following phases:

— Preliminary forms of a joint exercise of *episcopé* (chapter 6)

— Initial act of recognition (chapter 7)

— Collegial exercise of *episcopé* (chapter 8)

— Transition to a common ordained ministry (chapter 9).

---

[163] Cf. remarks on "recognition" and "reception" as "interrelated aims" (No. 49 above and Note 47).

119. It is of decisive importance for understanding and implementing this process that one attend to and preserve its integral and correlative character. It is not a matter of isolated acts or of phases in a gradual process. Rather the reciprocal recognition of ministries means essentially enabling and initiating the joint exercise of *episcopé* out of which then the ordained ministry arises. And therefore a mutual recognition of ministries which does not initiate the joint exercise of *episcopé* and the common ordained ministry growing out of it is insufficient for the realization of structured church fellowship. Furthermore, a joint exercise of *episcopé,* including ordaining, is inconceivable without the act of mutual recognition of the ministries, an act which by its nature enables and initiates the joint exercise of *episcopé.*

6. Preliminary Forms of the Joint Exercise of *Episcopé*

120. As a rule a preparatory process will be needed before the above-described correlative and integral process of mutual recognition of ministries and joint exercise of *episcopé* begins in its strict sense, a process during which a gradual recognition of ministries[164] and the appropriate prototypical forms of a joint exercise of ministries, especially the ministry of *episcopé,* are developed.

121. Such preliminary forms are, for example:

— working groups or Christian councils which already exist in many countries;

— mutual invitation of church leaders, pastors and laity to synods of the two churches, with a right to speak;

— development of more solid forms of working relationship, at the local or regional levels, between those who exercise *episcopé* in the two churches so that even now they can speak and act jointly where conscience does not require them to speak and act separately;

— creation in a country or a region of conciliar organs for the exchange of experiences and for common consultation in order to arrive at common decisions in such matters as evangelization, social service, public responsibility, etc.

122. Also in these preliminary forms or steps on the way to joint exercise of the *episcopé,* the main point will always be interrelating of both dimensions of the process, i.e., mutual recognition and joint exercise of the ministries, in which the participation and active cooperation of the entire ecclesial community should also be ensured.

---

[164] *The Ministry in the Church,* Nos. 74–86; especially Nos. 83–85.

7. Initial Act of Recognition

123. If a fundamental consensus is reached on faith, sacramental life and ordained ministry such that remaining differences between Catholics and Lutherans no longer can appear as church dividing, and reciprocal doctrinal condemnations no longer have any basis, then a mutual act of recognition should certainly follow.

124. This act entails a recognition of the fundamental consensus which is ecclesially binding and, at the same time, a mutual recognition that in the other church the church of Jesus Christ is actualized. It declares and confirms the will of both churches to relate to each other as churches of Jesus Christ and to live in full fellowship (*communio ecclesiarum*). Concerning the common ministry needed for full church fellowship, this means:

— on the Catholic side affirmation of the existence in the Lutheran churches of the ministry instituted by Christ in his church while at the same time pointing to a lack of fullness of the ordained ministry as a *defectus* which, for the sake of church fellowship, has jointly to be overcome;

— an enabling and concurrent authoritative beginning of a joint exercise of *episcopé* which progressively brings about and implies fellowship in the fully structured ordained ministry.

125. The act of recognition should be appropriate to the binding, ecclesial and integral character of the process of realizing church fellowship. To it belong a binding confessional declaration and an appropriate liturgical celebration in which, if possible, the first joint ordination should be held, thus marking the beginning of the joint exercise of *episcopé*.

Church fellowship begun in this manner opens possibilities of sacramental and particularly eucharistic fellowship, the modalities of which have to be clarified on the Catholic side according to the existing canon law.[165]

---

[165] Cf. particularly *The Code of Canon Law*, in English translation, London/Sydney, 1983, can. 844, paras. 1, 2 and 3, pp. 156f.
"1. Catholic ministers may lawfully administer the sacraments only to catholic members of Christ's faithful, who equally may lawfully receive them only from catholic ministers, except as provided in paras. 2, 3 and 4 of this canon and in can. 861, para. 2.
"2. Whenever necessity requires or a genuine spiritual advantage commends it, and provided the danger of error or indifferentism is avoided, Christ's faithful for whom it is physically or morally impossible to approach a catholic minister, may lawfully receive the sacraments of penance, the Eucharist and anointing of the sick from non-catholic ministers in whose Churches these sacraments are valid. ▶

126. Church fellowship between Catholics and Lutherans is ultimately sought as a fellowship between the whole Catholic Church and the totality of the Lutheran churches. Any act of initial recognition — whether it involves the churches at the local, regional, national or international levels — must have this as its goal.

On the Lutheran side, in view of these considerations, the relevant decisions would be taken by the independent churches (for example, *Landeskirchen* or national churches, or their associations). In this respect forms must be found which ensure that action is being taken in solidarity with the other churches of the Lutheran communion.

On the Catholic side note must be taken of the requirements of the episcopate as a whole. Depending on the circumstances at any given time local bishops, bishops of a church province or an episcopal conference would have to take primary responsibility. If a positive judgment is arrived at, the act of initial recognition must occur in cooperation with the Pope, because such an act concerns the whole Catholic Church. On the basis of his particular responsibility for the unity of Christians and the fellowship of the churches, it is the task of the Pope to approve or encourage such a local act in the name of the Catholic Church.

8. A Single *Episcopé* in Collegial Form

127. The common exercise of *episcopé,* including ordaining — made possible by the recognition of ministries —, through which community of faith and sacraments between Lutherans and Catholics becomes structured church fellowship, will initially take *the shape of a single episcopé exercised in collegial form.*

In places where they exist together the churches would provide for themselves a single episcopate in collegial form. It would go beyond all preliminary forms of parallel or partial joint exercise of *episcopé,* but without merging the two episcopates. This single episcopate would at the same time ensure necessary unity and legitimate diversity. What is foreseen is a form of local church in which our churches would truly be one without having been absorbed. This is the case, for example, with the united churches of the East (see Nos. 35–40 above), and is the intention

---

"3. Catholic ministers may lawfully administer the sacraments of penance, the Eucharist and anointing of the sick to members of the eastern Churches not in full communion with the catholic Church, if they spontaneously ask for them and are properly disposed. The same applies to members of other Churches which the Apostolic See judges to be in the same position as the aforesaid eastern Churches so far as the sacraments are concerned."

of the model of "unity in reconciled diversity" (see Nos. 31–34 above).[166] In such a situation, the Catholic or Lutheran congregations would preserve their existing links with their bishop. Moreover, the collegial exercise of *episcopé* in a region or a country can be furthered by the presence of a regional primate to whom his episcopal colleagues grant certain privileges, as for example, convening and chairing of an assembly, or under certain conditions, representation of the church of the region or country vis-à-vis civil authorities.[167]

128. Such a form of jointly exercised *episcopé* is most readily derived from the *ductus* of the preceding considerations, commends itself on the basis of the nature of the growing understanding and convergence between Catholics and Lutherans, and corresponds most clearly and honestly to the mutual recognition of ministries already set forth.

This form of jointly exercised *episcopé* is also in basic agreement with the understanding of the unity of the local church as it was held and practised in the Early Church:

The unity of the local church found expression in the Early Church through a single bishop exercising jurisdiction in one and the same territory.[168] The catholicity and apostolicity of the church as well as its unity was thus to be demonstrated and preserved.

Neither race nor language nor class nor any other human condition can be the principle of church unity. The "localness" of the church, linked with a single bishop, makes clear that thereby Christians are one with each other and that, on the basis of one faith and one baptism, they gather around one eucharist. This eucharist is always celebrated in unity with the bishop.

129. There are, therefore, multiple reasons for the traditional principle of a single bishop in one local church. However in a situation in which

---

[166] In connection with such a situation Pierre Duprey writes: "It is possible that what the Council of Chalcedon and tradition as a whole regarded as essential, that is that there should be one bishop in a single place, may be impossible to realize at least in the first stage — a stage which may be very long. But ... it is of capital importance to achieve the unity of *episcopé:* if it cannot be personal, it can be collegial" (*Mid-Stream,* vol. XVII, No. 4, October, 1978, p. 384).

[167] Some Lutheran churches, for example in Sweden and Finland, have an episcopal primate by established custom and consider this order as helpful. A resident bishop acting in concert with suffragans is a manner of exercising *episcopé* often encountered in the Catholic Church.

[168] Nicaea, c. 8 (COD, 9); Constantinople I, c. 2 (COD, 27–28); Lateran IV, c. 9 (COD, 215).

— as in ours — the concern is the realization of church fellowship between hitherto separated churches, forms of local church structure seem possible which ensure and testify to the unity, catholicity and apostolicity of these churches without in each case being presided over by only one single bishop.

130. That does not exclude the question whether, following the creation of the common ministry to which the jointly exercised *episcopé* would lead (see chapter 9 below), there can or shall be also other forms of jointly exercised *episcopé* than the collegial one (see chapter 10 below).

131. Whatever the precise procedures for the common exercise of *episcopé* may be, the nature and the content of the decisions to be taken must be subject to an evaluation process which could extend over several years. On the Catholic side, churches engaged in such a process must account before the whole Catholic Church for their initiatives, the difficulties encountered, and their positive experiences. Other Catholic churches, in contact with Lutheran churches somewhere in the world, will listen to them attentively. The indispensable discussion partner for them will be the Roman See because of its special role within the Catholic Church.

9. Transition from Joint Exercise of *Episcopé* to a Common Ordained Ministry

132. The joint exercise of the ministry of *episcopé,* which includes ordaining, leads to the gradual establishment of a common ordained ministry.

133. The formation of the ordained church ministry would be the result of individual ordinations which would take place whenever there is a candidate to ordain. All neighbouring bishops, Lutherans and Catholics, on the basis of the jointly exercised *episcopé* would ordain the new minister together. At the end of this process — within a reasonable space of time — the common ordained ministry would be realized.

134. Each of these ordinations must be understood and undertaken as an event which is at the same time (a) confessional, (b) epicletic, (c) communal and (d) juridical:

a. At the moment of taking up his ministry, the new minister confesses the apostolic faith before the entire worshipping community which, together with the Catholic and Lutheran bishops (or other ministers exercising *episcopé*) present on that occasion, witnesses to the correctness of his faith.

b. The entire action of ordination is embraced by the invocation of the Holy Spirit by the whole worshipping community.[169] Within this liturgical action the gift of the spirit, necessary for the exercise of the ministry, is imparted through the imposition of hands by the Catholic and Lutheran bishops.

c. Not everything, however, can depend on the common imposition of hands. The whole congregation is also involved. It could in one way or another participate in the election of the ordinand. As a rule, members of the church or congregation testify to the faith and morals of the candidate. The church or congregation for which the minister is being ordained, engages in an act of acceptance (reception). Finally, ordination also concerns the fellowship among the churches since it is one of the tasks of those ordained to further this fellowship.

d. Ordination sets one immediately into the service of the church and confers the authority inherent in such service. In the Catholic Church a new bishop has to be appointed or confirmed by the Pope. As various current concordats indicate, or as in the election of the patriarchs of the united churches of the East, the Catholic Church can adopt various procedures that do not necessarily eventuate in direct appointment.

135. It must be clearly understood that at stake in joint ordinations by Catholic and Lutheran bishops is a gift of grace of the Holy Spirit received in common by Catholics and Lutherans. In a confession of gratitude the two partners recognize together that the common and collegial ordained ministry is a gift of the Spirit to the apostolic church. At this juncture it would therefore be wrong to pose the question of what the one partner has given to the other.

136. A common ordained ministry would thus grow out of the jointly exercised *episcopé*. This transition would be a *process* which is so irrevocably rooted in a truly joint exercise of *episcopé* that, should it not take place or be discontinued, one could no longer really speak of a jointly exercised *episcopé*. Ordination constitutes one of the most important functions of *episcopé*.[170]

137. This transition to a common ordained ministry is pre-eminently a *gift of God*. Understood as epicletic and confessional events, the ordinations through which our churches receive the ministry show that this common ordained ministry also is not the result of human efforts, but God's gift given through God's Spirit.

---

[169] Hyppolytus, op.cit., No. 2, p. 33.
[170] Cf. *The Ministry in the Church,* Nos. 29, 43 and 44.

138. The *dimension of ecclesial reconciliation* inherent in this event should be expressed in all local congregations through preparation marked not only by joy and gratitude, but also by penitence; both sides confessing their sins against *koinonia*.

139. In this act of reconciliation and penitence, as is generally characteristic of the path we have proposed, our churches turn resolutely towards the future and leave it to God to judge the past. This implies that the time elapsing between the reciprocal recognition of ministries and the beginning of the jointly exercised *episcopé* on the one hand, and the establishing of the common ministry on the other be considered or declared a time of real but growing and deepening church fellowship. It is *a period of transition vouchsafed by God.*[171]

140. The form described here for realizing a common ordained ministry is not intended to exclude other forms. Rather, it appears to us to be the most appropriate one for the relationship between Lutheran churches and the Roman Catholic Church. In filling vacant posts by new ordinations one avoids problems which could encumber other procedures which have been discussed or could allow for misinterpretations:

a. *Reordination:* Its problems are not only terminological: one would properly speak of "ordination" in the case of an ordination considered null and void. Reordination is primarily a problem because the church whose ministers were newly ordained, would have to admit the invalidity of all previous ordinations.

b. *Supplementary Ordination:* In view of the fact that previous ordinations were intended for a particular church and not for the universal church, a "supplementary ordination" has been considered. The problem here is that existing ordinations are not then taken seriously. For the Catholic Church, therefore, a "supplementary ordination" is inconceivable when it recognizes the ordination of a previously separated church, as, for example, the Orthodox Church.

c. *Act of "reconciliation of ministries":* What is meant here is a comprehensive act of worship during which by mutual imposition of hands forgiveness is asked and the Holy Spirit is invoked in prayer that it would grant to all the gifts they need. The problematic of such

---

[171] Hesitations expressed in the BEM statement on the Ministry lose their point: Churches that are willing "to accept episcopal succession as a sign of the apostolicity of the life of the whole Church ... yet ... cannot accept any suggestion that the ministry exercised in their own tradition should be invalid until the moment that it enters into an existing line of episcopal succession" (No. 38).

a broad act of "reconciliation of ministries" derives from its ambiguity and, consequently, from its unclarity. Is there implicitly an ordination or a supplementary ordination? Is the validity of previous ordinations taken seriously?

d. *Mutual commissioning:* If previous ordinations in the other church are considered valid, a mutual commissioning of ordained ministers would be conceivable in order to achieve a common church ministry. The problematic here is that this would be a mere administrative act while the establishment of a ministerial fellowship cannot be reduced to a legal action. Moreover, mutual commissioning would be an act among ordained ministers with no attention to the role of the people of God.

141. For the transition period the way proposed makes it imperative to determine precisely the juridical status of the jointly ordained as well as of those bishops and ministers (presbyters) not yet jointly ordained.

10. Exercise of the Common Ordained Ministry

142. After the realization of a common ordained ministry, the exercise of the episcopate need not be uniform for each place. Specific historical, social and cultural situations, as well as the diversity of spiritual traditions, can speak in favour of exercising that ministry in different ways. According to local circumstances, one can imagine at least three forms of the exercise of the episcopate and, consequently, of a truly united local church:

143. First Form: *A Single Episcopé in Collegial Form*

In this case the mode of exercising the *episcopé,* already practised during the transition period, would be continued (see Nos. 119–122 above).

144. Second Form: *A Single Bishop for Differently Structured Parishes*

Parishes which differ on the basis of their spiritual and theological traditions live under one bishop who cares for the fellowship among them and also protects their legitimate differences. Thus in the united evangelical *Landeskirchen* of Germany, for example, there are Reformed and Lutheran parishes which have a common bishop or church president and are subject to a common church authority. Also Catholic Armenians or Maronites living under a bishop of the Latin rite have the possibility of maintaining their religious identity outside their native country by having their own parishes. In the framework of church fellowship a similar practice would be conceivable between Catholics and Lutherans.

145. Third Form: *Merger*

The churches unite into a single church in which the parishes are also merged. The merged church would have only a single bishop. This form which is foreseen, for example, by the model of "organic union" (see Nos. 16–18 above) seems legitimate and feasible — if it is desired — especially in the case of churches which live in a non-Christian environment.[172]

11. Indivisibility of the *Koinonia*

146. The realization of church fellowship in which community of faith and community in the sacraments attain ecclesial shape confronts both Lutherans and Catholics with the question of the indivisibility of the *koinonia,* even though the problem does not present itself in a completely symmetrical manner for the two sides.

147. From the Lutheran point of view: If a Lutheran church enters into full fellowship with the Catholic Church, it does not mean:

a. that this church enters *ipso facto* into fellowship with those churches which are already in fellowship with the Catholic Church;

b. that this Lutheran church forgoes *ipso facto* its fellowship with the other Lutheran churches and with other churches not in fellowship with the Catholic Church;

c. that the remaining Lutheran churches, in fellowship with this church but not with the Catholic Church, enter *ipso facto* into fellowship with the Catholic Church or renounce their fellowship with this church.[173]

But it does mean:

a. that for this church the question of fellowship with those churches which are in fellowship with the Catholic Church is raised on a new level, under new presuppositions and with greater urgency than previously;

b. that this church affirms as its task and responsibility working towards fellowship of all other Lutheran churches with the Catholic Church;

---

[172] Cf. the Statement concerning the attitude of the LWF to churches in Union Negotiations, *Sent Into the World,* op. cit., pp. 142f.

[173] Compare, for example, the situation that has been created by the establishment of church fellowship between Lutheran, United and Reformed churches in Europe — Leuenberg Agreement, 1973.

c. that the remaining Lutheran churches also consider and affirm the possibility of a fellowship with the Catholic Church as their own possibility to a greater extent than previously.

148. On the Catholic side this question arises: is it possible for the Catholic Church to be in full fellowship with a church which is itself in fellowship with another church with which the Catholic Church is not in fellowship?

Only a few insignificant historical precedents can be cited: in the Early Church, for example, perhaps the schism of Meletius of Antioch and the special position of Saint Basil; in more recent times (seventeenth/eighteenth century) fellowship with Orthodox church groups of the Greek islands without these churches becoming united churches. A remote analogy is the mutual admission to the eucharist in emergency situations by the Patriarchate of Moscow and the Catholic Church without this agreement being extended to the whole Orthodox Church.

Whatever historical precedents there may be, it is especially necessary to answer authoritatively the questions raised above. In doing so, it is assumed:

a. that the third church holds no doctrines which clearly contradict central truths of faith;

b. that, even if there is agreement in the central truths of faith, this church and its members are not admitted *ipso facto* to the eucharist in the whole Catholic Church.

Future Perspective

149. At the end of our description of how to achieve Catholic-Lutheran church fellowship many questions still remain open. The origins and the history of our ecclesial separation are too complex for us to be able to describe clearly and without ambiguity the process of overcoming it. Only as we continue along the road which we have started together will the obscurity disappear and answers be found to still open questions. We are sure to find in our churches many partners who will accompany us on this road with additions and corrections, encouragement and reassurance.

We hope to find also in other churches people who accompany us on this road. It could be that our reflections will help them just as we have received and continue to expect valuable impulses from them. Even as our efforts have their presuppositions in specific Catholic-Lutheran realities and have their goal in Catholic-Lutheran church fellowship, still we must not lose sight of the task and the aim of wider Christian unity. It is our deep conviction that each individual step towards unity must be understood as a step taken towards the unity of all churches.

This unity remains always "a blessing of the Triune God, a work which he accomplishes, by means he choses, in ways he determines".[174] Consciousness of that has been strengthened and deepened in us in the course of efforts to describe our common path. Seen in this way, all our reflections are a prayer to the Lord who knows ways which surpass our vision and are beyond our power.

---

[174] *Ways to Community,* No. 8.

List of Signatories

This document was signed by all members of the joint commission:

Roman Catholic Members

The Rt. Rev. H.L. Martensen (chairman)
The Rt. Rev. Dr. P.W. Scheele
Prof. Dr. J. Hoffmann
The Rev. Dr. J.F. Hotchkin
The Rev. Chr. Mhagama
Prof. Dr. St. Napiorkowski
Prof. Dr. V. Pfnür

Lutheran Members

Prof. Dr. G.A. Lindbeck (chairman)
The Rt. Rev. D.H. Dietzfelbinger (unable to attend)*
The Rev. Dr. K. Hafenscher
Drs. P. Nasution
The Rev. I.K. Nsibu
Prof. Dr. L. Thunberg
Prof. Dr. Bertoldo Weber

Consultants

Prof. Dr. H. Legrand OP (Roman Catholic)
Prof. Dr. H. Meyer (Lutheran)
Prof. Dr. H. Schütte (Roman Catholic)

Staff Members

The Rev. Dr. E.L. Brand (Lutheran World Federation)
P. Dr. P. Duprey PA (Secretariat for Promoting Christian Unity)
Msgr. Dr. A. Klein (Secretariat for Promoting Christian Unity)
The Rev. Dr. C.H. Mau, Jr. (Lutheran World Federation)

Rome, 3rd March 1984

---

* Bishop D. Hermann Dietzfelbinger died on 15th November 1984.

B.

Excursus

THE PRACTICE OF ORDINATION IN THE EARLY CHURCH
By Hervé Legrand O.P.

1. In considering the practice of ordination in the period of the early church fathers, all we are concerned to do in the present context is to point out the common ecclesiological structures on which that practice and its different forms are based. What is to be identified, therefore, is a *theological* model. Since the historical and social conditions of our churches today are wholly different from those of that remote era, there is no call to repristinate the past. Surely, however, considering it can stimulate creative reflection.

2. The ordination of a bishop is a complex process of which we shall emphasize here only those aspects which are most significant for the fellowship of the church.[1]

3. — With the participation of the bishops of neighbouring churches[2], the ordinand is chosen by the whole Christian people and the clergy of the church in question.[3] This responsibility of the

---

[1] Paralleling the appeal of *The Eucharist* to the basic actions of the eucharistic celebration, here too an attempt is made to emphasize the basic features of the act of ordination to the degree that these reflect the interrelationships between the understanding of ministry and the conception of the church.

[2] Nicaea, can. 4 (COD 6–7).

[3] The rule given in the *Apostolic Tradition* of Hippolytus (No 2) is: "Let the bishop be ordained after he has been chosen by all the people" (*The Apostolic Tradition of Hippolytus*, Archon Books, Ann Arbor, Michigan, 1962, p. 33). Hippolytus' *Apostolic Tradition* is an important witness not only in virtue of its antiquity (about 220 AD) but also because of its later reception in the ecumenical movement. In the ordination of bishops in the East, this ritual was adopted from a very early date (Western Syria, Egypt and later at our time Ethiopia); in the Latin Church it forms the basis for the new rite of episcopal ordination after the Second Vatican Council; various Protestant churches, in particular the Episcopal Church in the USA and the United Methodist Church in the USA, have made it the pattern for their episcopal ordination services.

congregation in the choice of its bishop has a pneumatological basis: the person chosen by the local church is held to have been chosen by the Holy Spirit.[4] This active cooperation of people and bishops in the election and ordination shows that it is perfectly possible to combine the "congregational" and "episcopal" principles in the fellowship of the church.[5]

4. — At the inauguration of the new bishop into the apostolic ministry, an attestation of his orthodoxy in faith is required both by the

---

Following the reign of the emperor Constantine, the church in the East experienced a diminution of the active participation of the local church in electing its bishop; thus canon 4 of the Council of Nicaea refers only to the cooperation of the neighbouring bishops in the act of consecration. In the West, the local church preserved an active initiating role (this was later interrupted because of the migration of peoples), as is attested by the well-known election of Ambrose of Milan (Paulin, Vit. Ambr. 6, PL 14, 31) and that of Martin of Tours (Sulp. Severus, Vit. Martini 9, *Sources chrétiennes* 133, pp. 270–273). This active initiatory role of the local church was still defended in the fifth century by the bishops of Rome. For example, Celestine: "Nullus invitis detur episcopus. Cleri, plebis et ordinis, consensum ac desiderium requiratur" [No bishop should be appointed against the wishes of the faithful. Agreement and wish of the clergy, the people and the ordained ministry should be obtained.] (Epist. 4,5; Pl 50, 434); similarly St. Leo the Great: "He who is to be in charge of all should be chosen by all" (*Letters,* Washington DC, 1957, p. 44; Epist. 10,6; Pl 54, 634); and again: "No one, of course, is to be consecrated against the wishes of the people and without their requesting it" (ibid., p. 63; Epist. 14,5; PL 54, 673). In all cases it is not a question, of course, of the individual votes of the faithful in the sense of a modern political election; but to reduce the role of the local church to a mere consent by acclamation would not correspond to the facts.

[4] The term "vox populi, vox Dei" seems to have originated in the election to the ordained ministry. According to Cyprian, God with whom the real decision lies speaks through the voice of the people (Epist. 43,1; 55,8; 59,5; 68,2). Cf. on this: T. Osawa, "Das Bischofseinsetzungsverfahren bei Cyprian. Historische Untersuchungen zu den Begriffen *iudicium, suffragium, testimonium, consensus*", *Europäische Hochschulschriften* XXIII, 178, Frankfurt/Bern 1983. In the view of the author — following Cyprian — the people, as distinct from the clergy, had no right to cooperate actively and to take the initiative in the election.

[5] Cyprian could therefore write: "The bishop is in the Church and the Church is in the bishop" (*Letters 1–81,* Washington DC, 1964, p. 229; Epist. 66,8). The appointment of a bishop is subject to the condition that he is accepted by the local church. Canon 18 of the Council of Ancyra (AD 314) stipulates that a bishop is to be content with the rank of a presbyter if he is not accepted. If he is not prepared to do so, he is deposed. Canon 2147, para. 2,2 of the CIC of 1917 regards acceptance as necessary for the ministers (cf. also can. 1741, 3 of the CIC of 1983).

local Christians and the neighbouring bishops.[6] The apostolicity of the local church and of the whole church as well as the apostolicity of the ministry are integral elements in the fellowship of the church.

5. — Even if already elected, the ordinand does not become bishop without the cooperation of the leaders of the neighbour churches.[7] This shows that church fellowship requires catholicity.

6. — His reception by the other bishops as a colleague into one and the same office shows that the collegiality of the bishops is an expression of the fellowship between the churches.

7. — In the setting of the *epiklesis* of the whole assembly and with the imposition of hands by the bishops, he receives the gift of the Spirit.[8] The ordination takes place, therefore, within the *koinonia* in which the bishops and the congregation are united by the Holy Spirit.

8. — This gift is the particular charisma of presiding over his church (*pneuma hegemonikon*).[9] Ordination thus sets the bishop vis-à-vis his church. Even so he exercises this personal office in cooperation with a variety of gifts, charismata and ministries, all of which are given to the church by the Spirit.

9. — The charisma he receives enables him to assume his ministry and perform it with authority. The canonical aspect is inseparable

---

[6] The chief witnesses for a scrutiny of the bishop in the presence of the people are: Apostolic Tradition, 2; Const. Apost. VIII, 4,2,6; Cyprian, Epist. 38,1; Letter of the Nicene Council to the Egyptians 7–10, *Urkunden zur Geschichte des Arianischen Streites,* Berlin/Leipzig, 1935 — Works of Athanasius III, 1, 49–50; *Statuta Ecclesiae Antiqua,* cf. Ch. Munier, ed. Paris, 1960, 75–76.

[7] According to canon 4 of the Council of Nicaea, among the neighbouring bishops it is the responsibility of the Metropolitan to confirm such a procedure in his province. In this spirit, the Popes, as Metropolitans of the Roman province and as Primates of Italy, reserved to themselves the consecration of bishops from the beginning of the seventh century onwards. They were thus able to control the quality of the elections as carried out by the local churches. Only from the time when the Popes resided in Avignon (14th/15th centuries) did they try to appoint all the Latin bishops. The CIC of 1917 was the first to turn this into a universal principle (cf. can. 329, para. 2: "The Supreme Pontiff freely appoints them" [the bishops], a formula, which was taken up again with an enlarged addition in CIC of 1983, can. 377, para. 1: "or confirms those lawfully elected" [*The Code of Canon Law,* in English translation, London/Sydney, 1983, p. 66; cf. can. 329, para. 2]).

[8] Hippolytus, op. cit., p. 33: "All indeed shall keep silent, praying in their heart for the descent of the Spirit."

[9] Ibid., No. 3, pp. 34f.

from the pneumatological aspect: canon law is an integral element of the fellowship of the church.

10. — The local church celebrates the ordination of its bishop in the context of a eucharistic assembly over which the newly ordained bishop presides. This points to the close connection between church fellowship and eucharistic communion and to the responsibility for both inherent in the office.

11. — The ordination of the bishop is always celebrated on the Sunday, the day on which the resurrection and the outpouring of the Spirit at Pentecost are commemorated, thereby bringing the eschatological dimension of the ministry and Christian communion to expression in ordination.[10] In his ministry, therefore, the bishop is to represent the inner connection between Christ's apostolically attested act of salvation, the actualizing of the apostolic witness to Christ, and the expected return of the Lord Jesus Christ.

---

[10] Cf. Th. Michels, *Beiträge zur Geschichte des Bischofsweihetages im christlichen Altertum und im Mittelalter,* LQF 22, Münster, 1927.

C.

Martin Luther — Witness to Jesus Christ

Statement by the Roman Catholic/Lutheran Joint Commission on the occasion of Martin Luther's 500th birthday.

PREFACE

In their effort to find ways to community in faith and to understand and surmount existing differences at their very roots, the Roman Catholic/ Lutheran Joint Commission studied frequently the Reformation and the person and work of Martin Luther. On the occasion of the 450th anniversary of the Confessio Augustana, the Commission affirmed the fact that we are "all under one Christ" and are able to join together in common witness to basic doctrinal truths.

The 500th anniversary of the birth of Martin Luther provided the occasion to reflect on him and what he sought to do, and to publish a joint statement which should assist in reconciliation and understanding. Its purpose is to emphasize some central concerns of Luther and to bring out his ecumenical significance, to draw attention to the new understanding resulting from Lutheran and Catholic studies and in this way to help overcome a picture of Luther which in former times was often disorted.

Kloster Kirchberg, 6th May 1983

Hans L. Martensen
Bishop of Copenhagen
Denmark

George A. Lindbeck
Professor, Yale University
USA

co-chairmen

I. FROM CONFLICT TO RECONCILIATION

1. This year our churches celebrate the 500th anniversary of the birth of Martin Luther. Christians, whether Protestant or Catholic, cannot disregard the person and the message of this man. Standing on the threshold of modern times, he has had, and still has a crucial influence on the history of the church, of society and of thought.

2. For centuries opinions about Luther were diametrically opposed to one another. Catholics saw him as the personification of heresy and blamed him as the fundamental cause of schism between the western churches. Already in the 16th century the Protestants began to glorify Luther as a religious hero and not infrequently also as a national hero. Above all, however, Luther was often regarded as the founder of a new church.

3. The judgment of Luther was closely connected with each church's view of the other: they accused one another of abandoning the true faith and the true church.

4. In the churches of the Reformation and in theology, the rediscovery of Luther began in the early days of this century. Soon afterwards, intensive study of the person of Luther and his work started on the Catholic side. This study has made notable scholarly contributions to Reformation and Luther research and, together with the growing ecumenical understanding, has paved the way towards a more positive Catholic attitude to Luther. We see on both sides a lessening of outdated, polemically coloured images of Luther. He is beginning to be honoured in common as a witness to the gospel, a teacher in the faith and a herald of spiritual renewal.

5. The recent celebrations of the 450th anniversary of the Augsburg Confession (1980) have made an essential contribution to this perspective. This confession of faith is inconceivable without the person and theology of Luther. Furthermore the insight that the Augsburg Confession reflects "a full accord on fundamental and central truths" (Pope John Paul II, 17th November 1980) between Catholics and Lutherans facilitates the common affirmation of fundamental perceptions of Luther.

6. Luther's call for church reform, a call to repentance, is still relevant for us. He summons us to listen anew to the gospel, to recognize our own unfaithfulness to the gospel and to witness credibly to it. This cannot happen today without attention to the other church and to its witness and without the surrender of polemical stereotypes and the search for reconciliation.

II. WITNESS TO THE GOSPEL

7. In criticizing various aspects of the theological tradition and church life of his time, Luther considered himself a witness to the gospel — an "unworthy evangelist of our Lord Jesus Christ". He appealed to the biblical apostolic testimony which, as a "doctor of Holy Scripture", he was committed to interpret and proclaim. He took his stand consciously on the confession of the Early Church to the Triune God and to Christ's person and work, and saw in this confession an authoritative expression of the biblical message. In his striving for reformation, which brought him external persecution and inner tribulation, he found assurance and comfort in his call by the church to study and teach the Scriptures. In this conviction he felt himself supported by the Lord of the church himself.

8. Knowing his responsibility as a teacher and pastor, and at the same time personally experiencing the anguished need for faith, he was led by his intense study of the Scriptures to a renewed discovery of God's mercy in the midst of the fears and uncertainties of his time. According to his own testimony, this "Reformation discovery" consisted in recognizing that God's righteousness is, in the light of Romans 1:17, a bestowal of righteousness, not a demand that condemns the sinner. "He who through faith is righteous shall live", i.e., he lives by the mercy granted by God through Christ. In this discovery, confirmed for Luther by the church father Augustine, the message of the Bible became a joyful message, that is, "gospel". It opened for him, as he said, "the gate of paradise".

9. In his writings, as in his preaching and teaching, Luther became a witness to this liberating message. As the "doctrine of the justification of the sinner through faith alone", it was the central point of his theological thinking and of his exegesis of Scripture. Those whose consciences suffered under the dominion of the law and human ordinances, and who were tormented by their failures and by concern for eternal salvation could gain assurance through faith in the gospel of the liberating promise of God's grace.

10. Historical research has shown that the beginnings of an agreement on this fundamental concern of Luther's were already apparent in the theological discussions at the time of the Reformation. But this agreement was not effectively accepted by either side, and was obscured and nullified by later polemics.

11. In our time, Luther research and biblical studies on both sides have again opened the way for a mutual understanding of the central concerns of the Lutheran Reformation. Awareness of the historical conditioned-

ness of all forms of expression and thought has contributed to the widespread recognition among Catholics that Luther's ideas, particularly on justification, are a legitimate form of Christian theology. Thus in summarizing what had already been jointly affirmed by Catholic and Lutheran theologians in 1972 ("The Gospel and the Church"), the Catholic-Lutheran statement on the Augsburg Confession says that: "A broad consensus emerges in the doctrine of justification, which was decisively important for the Reformation (CA IV): it is solely by grace and by faith in Christ's saving work and not because of any merit in us that we are accepted by God and receive the Holy Spirit who renews our hearts and equips us for and calls us to good works" ("All Under One Christ", 1980).

12. As witness to the gospel, Luther proclaimed the biblical message of God's judgment and grace, of the scandal and the power of the cross, of the lostness of human beings and of God's act of salvation. As an "unworthy evangelist of our Lord Jesus Christ" Luther points beyond his own person in order to confront us all the more inescapably with the promise and the claim of the gospel he confessed.

III. CONFLICT AND THE SCHISM IN THE CHURCH

13. Luther's interpretation and preaching of justification by faith alone came into conflict with the prevailing forms of piety which obscured God's gift of righteousness. Luther believed that his protests were in conformity with the teaching of the church and, indeed, even defended that teaching. Any thought of dividing the church was far from his mind and was strongly rejected by him. But there was no understanding for his concerns among the ecclesiastical and theological authorities either in Germany or in Rome. The years following the famous "95 Theses" of 1517 were marked by increasing polemics. As the disputes intensified, Luther's primarily religious concerns were increasingly intertwined with questions of church authority and were also submerged by questions of political power. It was not Luther's understanding of the gospel considered by itself which brought about conflict and schism in the church, but rather the ecclesial and political concomitants of the Reformation movement.

14. When Luther was threatened with excommunication and summoned to revoke what for him were essential theological convictions, he saw in this the refusal of the secular and church authorities to discuss his theological reasoning. The conflict turned more and more on the question of final authority in matters of faith. Luther appealed to Scripture

in this dispute, and came to doubt that all doctrinal decisions of the Popes and councils were binding in conscience. Yet his emphasis on the *sola scriptura* and on the clarity of Scripture included acceptance of the creeds of the Early Church and respect for traditions which were in accordance with Scripture. He maintained throughout all conflicts his trust in God's promise to keep his church in the truth.

15. As the hostility of the church authorities increased, so did Luther's polemical attitude. The Pope was rejected as "Antichrist", the mass condemned as idolatry. In turn, Luther and his followers were categorized as heretics and sometimes even accused of apostasy. The hope that agreement could be reached at the Diet in Augsburg in 1530 was not fulfilled. Luther considered the rejection he met with as a sign of the approaching apocalypse. He could see no way back from the attitude of reciprocal condemnation.

16. Luther was claimed by a great variety of groups and tendencies in church and society in pursuit of their special interests (anti-clerical, revolutionary or enthusiast). He himself fought against these pressures, but his image suffered from distortions which still persist to this day.

17. These historical events cannot be reversed or undone. We can, however, seek to remove their negative consequences by investigating their origins and admitting culpable failures. Ultimately, however, they will only be healed when the positive aims of the Reformation become the joint concern of Lutherans and Roman Catholics.

IV. RECEPTION OF REFORMATION CONCERNS

18. The Lutheran churches have tried over the centuries to conserve Luther's theological and spiritual insights. Not all his writings, however, have influenced the Lutheran churches to the same degree. There has often been a tendency to give more importance to his polemical works than to his pastoral and theological writings. Those writings which were given the status of confessional documents are of special ecclesial significance. Among these, his two catechisms occupy a special position in the life of the churches. Together with the Confessio Augustana, they form an appropriate basis for an ecumenical dialogue.

19. Nevertheless, Luther's heritage has suffered various losses and distortions in the course of history.

— The Bible was increasingly isolated from its church context, and its authority was legalistically misunderstood because of the doctrine of verbal inspiration;

- Luther's high estimate of sacramental life was largely lost during the Enlightenment and in pietism;

- Luther's concept of human beings as persons before God was misinterpreted as individualism;

- the message of justification was at times displaced by moralism;

- his reservations about the role of political authorities in church leadership were silenced for long periods of time, and

- his doctrine of the twofold nature of God's rule (the doctrine of "the Two Kingdoms") was misused to legitimate the church's denial of responsibility for social and political life.

20. Together with their gratitude for Luther's contributions, Lutheran churches are in our day aware of his limitations in person and work and of certain negative effects of his actions. They cannot approve his polemical excesses; they are aghast at the anti-Jewish writings of his old age; they see that his apocalyptic outlook led him to judgments which they cannot approve, e.g., on the papacy, the Anabaptist movement and the Peasants' War. In addition, certain structural weaknesses in Lutheran churches have become obvious, especially in the way in which their administration was taken over by princes or the state — which Luther himself wanted to think of as simply an emergency arrangement.

21. A defensive attitude towards Luther and his thinking was in some respect determinative for the Roman Catholic Church and its development since the Reformation. Fear of the distribution of editions of the Bible unauthorized by the church, a centralizing over-emphasis on the papacy and a onesidedness in sacramental theology and practice were deliberately developed features of Counter-Reformation Catholicism. On the other hand, some of Luther's concerns are taken into account in such Tridentine reforming efforts as for example, the renewal of preaching, the intensification of religious instruction and the emphasis on the Augustinian doctrine of grace.

22. There has developed in our century — first of all in German-speaking areas — an intensive Catholic re-evaluation of Luther the man and of his Reformation concerns. It is widely recognized that he was justified in attempting to reform the theology and the abuses in the church of his time and that his fundamental belief — justification given to us by Christ without any merit of our own — does not in any way contradict genuine Catholic tradition, such as is found, for example, in Saint Augustine and Thomas Aquinas.

23. This new attitude to Luther is reflected in what Cardinal Willebrands said at the Lutheran World Federation's Fifth Assembly: "Who ... would still deny that Martin Luther was a deeply religious person who

with honesty and dedication sought for the message of the gospel? Who would deny that in spite of the fact that he fought against the Roman Catholic Church and the Apostolic See — and for the sake of truth one must not remain silent about this — he retained a considerable part of the old Catholic faith? Indeed, is it not true that the Second Vatican Council has even implemented requests which were first expressed by Martin Luther, among others, and as a result of which many aspects of Christian faith and life now find better expression than they did before? To be able to say this in spite of all the differences is a reason for great joy and much hope."

24. Among the insights of the Second Vatican Council which reflect elements of Luther's concerns may be numbered:

— an emphasis on the decisive importance of Holy Scripture for the life and teaching of the church (Dogmatic Constitution on Divine Revelation);

— the description of the church as "the people of God" (Dogmatic Constitution on the Church, chapter II);

— the affirmation of the need for continued renewal of the church in its historical existence (Dogmatic Constitution on the Church, 8; Decree on Ecumenism, 6);

— the stress on the confession of faith in the cross of Jesus Christ and of its importance for the life of the individual Christian and of the church as a whole (Dogmatic Constitution on the Church, 8; Decree on Ecumenism, 4; Pastoral Constitution on the Church in the Modern World, 37);

— the understanding of church ministries as service (Decree on the Bishops' Pastoral Office in the Church, 16; Decree on the Ministry and Life of Priests);

— the emphasis on the priesthood of all believers (Dogmatic Constitution on the Church, 10 and 11; Decree on the Apostolate of the Laity, 2–4);

— commitment to the right of the individual to liberty in religious matters (Declaration on Religious Freedom).

25. There are also other requests of Luther which can be regarded as fulfilled in the light of contemporary Catholic theology and church practice: the use of the vernacular in the liturgy; the possibility of communion in both kinds, and the renewal of the theology and celebration of the eucharist.

V. LUTHER'S LEGACY AND OUR COMMON TASK

26. It is possible for us today to learn from Luther together. "In this we could all learn from him that God must always remain the Lord, and that our most important human answer must always remain absolute confidence in God and our adoration of him" (Cardinal Willebrands).

— As a theologian, preacher, pastor, hymn-writer, and man of prayer, Luther has with extraordinary spiritual force witnessed anew to the biblical message of God's gift of liberating righteousness and made it to shine forth.

— Luther directs us to the priority of God's word in the life, teaching and service of the church.

— He calls us to a faith which is absolute trust in the God who in the life, death and resurrection of his son has shown himself to be gracious to us.

— He teaches us to understand grace as a personal relationship of God to human beings which is unconditional and frees from fear of God's wrath and for service of one another.

— He testifies that God's forgiveness is the only basis and hope for human life.

— He calls the churches to constant renewal by the word of God.

— He teaches us that unity in essentials allows for differences in customs, order and theology.

— He shows us as a theologian how knowledge of God's mercy reveals itself only in prayer and meditation. It is the Holy Spirit who persuades us of the truth of the gospel and keeps and strengthens us in that truth in spite of all temptations.

— He exhorts us to remember that reconciliation and Christian community can only exist where not only "the rule of faith" is followed, but also the "rule of love", "which thinks the best of everyone, is not suspicious, believes the best about its neighbours and calls anyone who is baptized a saint" (Luther).

27. Trust and reverent humility before the mystery of God's mercy are expressed in Luther's last confession which, as his spiritual and theological last will and testament, can serve as a guide in our common search for unifying truth: "We are beggars. This is true."

List of Signatories

This document was signed by all members of the joint commission:

Roman Catholic Members

The Rt. Rev. H.L. Martensen (chairman)
The Rt. Rev. Dr. P.W. Scheele
Prof. Dr. J. Hoffmann
The Rev. Dr. J.F. Hotchkin
The Rev. Chr. Mhagama
Prof. Dr. St. Napiorkowski
Prof. Dr. V. Pfnür

Lutheran Members

Prof. Dr. G.A. Lindbeck (chairman)
The Rt. Rev. D.H. Dietzfelbinger (unable to attend)
The Rev. Dr. K. Hafenscher
Drs. P. Nasution
The Rev. I.K. Nsibu
Prof. Dr. L. Thunberg
Prof. Dr. Bertoldo Weber

Consultants

Prof. Dr. H. Legrand OP (Roman Catholic)
Prof. Dr. H. Meyer (Lutheran)
Prof. Dr. H. Schütte (Roman Catholic)
Prof. Dr. Vilmos Vajta (Lutheran)

Staff Members

P. Dr. P. Duprey PA (Secretariat for Promoting Christian Unity)
The Rev. Dr. Günther Gassmann (Lutheran World Federation)
Msgr. Dr. A. Klein (Secretariat for Promoting Christian Unity)
The Rev. Dr. C.H. Mau, Jr. (Lutheran World Federation)

Kloster Kirchberg (Württemberg), 6th May 1983